CW01632626

THE PLACE NAMES OF ELGINSHIRE;

THE PLACE NAMES OF ELGINSHIRE;

Donald Matheson

General Books

www.General-Books.net

Publication Data:

Title: The Place Names of Elginshire
Author: Donald Matheson
General Books publication date: 2009
Original publication date: 1905
Original Publisher: E. MacKay
Subjects: Names, Geographical
English language
Names, Geographical Scotland Elginshire
History / Europe / Great Britain
Language Arts Disciplines / Etymology

How We Made This Book
We automated the typing, proof reading and design of this book using Optical Character Recognition (OCR) software on a scanned copy of the original rare book. That allowed us to keep your cost as low as possible.
If the book is very old, worn and the type is faded, this can result in a lot of typos or missing text. This is also why our books don't have illustrations; the OCR software can't distinguish between an illustration and a smudge.
We understand how annoying typos, missing text or illustrations can be. That's why we provide a free digital copy of most books exactly as they were originally published. Simply go to our website (www.general-books.net) to check availability. And we provide a free trial membership in our book club so you can get free copies of other editions or related books.
OCR is not a perfect solution but we feel it's more important to make the book available for a low price than not at all. So we warn readers on our website and in the descriptions we provide to book sellers that our books don't have illustrations and may have typos or missing text. We also provide excerpts from each book to book sellers and on our website so you can preview the quality of the book before buying it.
If you would prefer that we manually type, proof read and design your book so that it's perfect, we are happy to do that. Simply contact us via our website for the cost.

Limit of Liability/Disclaimer of Warranty:
The publisher and author make no representations or warranties with respect to the accuracy or completeness of the book. The advice and strategies in the book may not be suitable for your situation. You should consult with a professional where appropriate. The publisher is not liable for any damages resulting from the book.
Please keep in mind that the book was written long ago; the information is not current. Furthermore, there may be typos, missing text or illustration and explained above.

CONTENTS

SECTION 1

The Royal Burgh of Elgin bears Argent, Sanctus Egidius habited in his robes and mytred holding in his dexter hand a pastoral staff and in his left hand a clasped book all proper: supported by two angels proper winged or volant upwards : and the motto " Sic itur ad astra" upon ane compartment suitabill to a Burgh Royal and for their colours red and white: recorded in terms of an interlocutor of Lyon King of Arms of 28th November, 1888, and agreeably to the blazon of James Skene, Lyon Depute of Date gth October, 1678.

St. Egidius, or Giles, was an abbot of the seventh century, and an Athenian by birth. He is said to have migrated to France, and to have spent several years of his life in the wild desert near the mouth of the Rhone, and subsequently in a forest in the diocese of Nismes, where the hunted animal with the arrow in its left shoulder came up to him tor refuge. St. Egidius died in the beginning of the eighth century, and his remains were removed to Tolouse, where they were deposited in the church of St. Saturnius.

ILLUSTRATIONS.

FACING PAGE

 INTRODUCTORY NOTICE.

THE aborigines of Scotland were clans of the same Gaelic origin as those who in early ages settled in England, and at the time of the Roman invasion under Agricola, they were in a similar condition to those of England. Scotland, from the Tweed and Eden on the south, to the Pentland Firth on the north, was divided among twenty-one tribes. Those on the east coast, owing to the greater fertility of the soil and drier climate, were more numerous and powerful than those on the west coast; but all of them, in accordance with Celtic customs, were independent of one another, and only co-operated under pressure of outward danger. Of these, the *Vacomagi* occupied the country from the Deveron on the east to the Beauly river on the west, comprehending Banffshire, Elginshire, Nairnshire, and the eastern portion of Inverness-shire, or the territories on the south of the Moray Firth or *Sinus Vararia* of the Romans. Their towns were: – *Ptoroton,* the *A lata Castra* of Ptolemy, now Burghead; *Tuessis* – Old Fochabers on the Spey; and *Tamia,* supposed to be Cullen; and *Eanatia,* supposed to be Banff. The *Vacomagi* were so denominated because they occupied these shores, from the old British word, *Vac,* a bay or firth – a word which runs through all the branches of the Aryan languages : Sanscrit, *vefa;* Greek, *oikos;*Polish, *wies;* Irish, *fich;* Welsh, *quic*; Gaelic, *uig;* and also the British word, *magh,* a plain. This is a root of great antiquity, and in the Latinised form, *magus,* is frequently used in the ancient place names of Gaul, as *Caesar-o-magus, Drus-o-magus, Novi-o- magus,* and *Rigio-magus.*

These tribes appear to have been little raised, at the time when history introduces them to our notice, above the condition of savages, but they were brave, alert, and had remarkable powers of enduring fatigue, cold, and famine, and Dio tells us they were literal democrats, acting as clans, and adopting any public measure only by common consent. Their vessels consisted of *curracha* or *coracles* – boats made of twigs and covered with skins. Thus they were until the year 140 A. D., when Lollius Urbicus was deputed to reduce them to obedience to Rome. It is said he reduced the country up to the Beauly Firth, the district from which southward to the Wall of Antoninus he called Vespasiana. In the year 306, while still under Roman influence, we find a new native name other than Britons given to the inhabitants of Scotland. Irish history informs us that the " Picts" were driven out of that country by the brave Milesians, when they took ships to *Cruith- an-tuath,* the old name for Scotland, and that their leader, Cathluan, obtained the sovereignty of the country, and was the first monarch of a long line of seventy kings. We can only accept this as a mere conjecture, as there is little doubt that the Picts were no other than a part of the race of ancient Caledonians under another name. Little is known of Pictish history for more than a hundred years after the Romans finally surrendered Britain, further than that some old chronicles give a list of the Pictish kings. By the accession of Bredi, the thirteenth king, in 586, to the Pictish throne, some light is let in on the darkness whichsurrounded the history of previous kings by his conversion to Christianity. He not only was converted himself, but was the means of making his people embrace the same faith. This, though proud of his many victories, was his greatest glory. The battles of the Pictish kings were with the Scoto-Irish from .

Dalriada, but the greatest of all was that fought at Dun-Nechtan, JHrYf , in 685, between a later Bredi and Egfrid, one of

the Saxon princes of Northumbria, who crossed Bernicia, or river Forth, penetrated through the defiles of Perth and Aberdeen, until his career was ended by his annihilation at Dun-Nechtan, now Dunnichen, where he and the majority of his soldiers fell. In 710 the Picts were finally defeated by the Saxons, who returned to the conquest under a new leader.

Up to this period the pirate or Vikingr of the northern seas confined his ravages to the countries south of the Baltic, but in 787 he appeared on the northern shores of England, and a few years after on the Caledonian shores. But it was not until 83D and following years that he entered the territory of the Pictish king, along the Moray Firth, where murderous conflicts between the fierce Norsemen, on the one hand, and Uen, the son of Ungus, and Bran, his brother, on the other, took place, with fatal results to the Picts. These events hastened the downfall of the Pictish monarchy. The Scottish king, Kenneth, carried into execution, in the year 843, the project he had long entertained of uniting the Scots and Picts, and placing both crowns on one head. For long after the union of the two crowns, the two races were recognised as distinct people, until in the 12th century they lost their characteristic distinctions by amalgamation with their conquerors. They were races of common origin and cognate speech, consequently they coalesced the more easily. The union increased

the power of both, and by the ascendancy of the Scots, their name was given to the whole of the northern part of Britain. The Scottish period extended from this union in 843 till the death of Donald Bane in 1097. During this period the Gaelic Scots predominated, and their language, being the same as that of the Picts, was universal throughout the country. From 1097 to 1306 a new people appears, " a new dynasty ascended the throne, a new jurisprudence generally prevailed, new ecclesiastical establishments were settled, and new manners and a new speech overspread the land." The fusion of the Celtic and Saxon races was a social conquest, and its results were to almost suppress the Celtic tongue and Celtic manners, or imprison them within the fastnesses of the Highlands.

It is now generally acknowledged that the Celts originally came from the East. They were, undoubtedly, the primitive inhabitants of Gaul, Belgium, and the British Isles, and their history has to be built up of the fragments we find scattered here and there in the form of ancient tradition, the discoveries of the spade and pick-axe, and above all by the traces of their original language found in the etymology of the names still attached to places, and monuments of undoubted Celtic origin. We find the primaeval names given to places in our own country in the original language appearing through the subsequent strata laid in various times, and the variations of spelling from the original root which have followed. Mallet says – " All Celtic nations have been accustomed to the worship of the sun" whose name in the Sanskrit, Hebrew, Greek, Norse, and Celtic languages is frequently met with. Laertius places the Druids of ancient Britain on an equality with the Chaldeans, and the Magi of Persia in point of learning and literature. Hence we may at once dispel the ideathat names were given to the hills, rivers, and fields in a haphazard manner, or that the mass of our place-names are derived from the Saxon speech. It is evident from Ptolemy's Geography of Britain, and from the Itinerary of Antoninus, that many places bore Celtic names merely altered by Latin terminations and English garb. We find a good example of this in the name Ptoroton, or now Burgbead, which before the circumnavigation of Britain by the Romans was *Tor-an-duin,* the fort on the headland; Ben Cruachan was *Pen-o-Crucium.* From these and many other examples that might be given there are strong grounds for believing that the great majority of the place names were given by its earliest occupants, handed down to us with the alterations introduced by writing and spelling which have, more than anything, changed and obscured the original term, but, notwithstanding, are still capable of being traced back to their original etymon. This involves labour, and the surest way in which it can be done is by finding out the primary orthography from which alone can the signification of a word be even approximately determined. In Scotland, and particularly throughout the county of Elgin, a large number of names can be interpreted as they are found by any one acquainted with the laws of transmutation of words. Elginshire names present many peculiarities, and have to be traced to the original through the three strata of English, Norse, and finally Gaelic. In their present form they are to be regarded from the phonetic standpoint, having been put down as they had been spoken, not as written in the original, and are in consequence materially corrupted. They are therefore of some importance from an ethnological as well as from a philological point of view.

" The ethnology of the ancient Britons has given rise to so muchdisputation that it is impossible to form any clear idea as to either their origin, physical features, manners, or religion, but of their language we are sure." Throughout Elginshire there is a large number of old records which contain the orthography of many of the names as written in mediaeval times. It is thus the most important of all sources of information on this interesting subject, as embodying very approximately, if not the original form, at least the original sound, now for the most part strange and meaningless to other than the student of place names. The next important source of information is local pronunciation, which is, however, of no use in the lower part of this county on account of its being lost in the all-prevailing doric from which the Celtic aspiration has completely disappeared – Inver-aven, anciently, *Inbhir-amhuinn* is now sounded Inner-an. This dropping of the aspiration throughout almost the whole of the county presents many difficulties which can only be removed by an appeal to old records and to the configuration of the place.

The majority of Elginshire place names are compound words, made up of a substantive and qualifying word or words, as *Tulach- min,* the smooth hillside; the qualifying word, as in many languages, coming after the substantive, and in several instances made up of two or more substantives, as Kintrae – *Ceann-traigh,* the shore head. In such words the emphasis usually falls upon the qualifying word; and, remembering this, it is of considerable assistance in the explication of words. Phonetic changes have been frequent and peculiar, because every new sound was in a direction further removed from the original, of which a good example is found in the word Urquhart.

Adamnan wrote it *Airchartdan;* the next form is *Orchartan,* then *Orcharden,* then Orchard, then *Urchard,* and finally *Urquhart,* signifying thetribal territory, and in which, through its various forms, the original pronunciation has been to a great extent preserved. In reducing these old names to modern form the inevitable result was the omission of the aspirates and the dropping out of the Celtic consonants, as a natural consequence of the Saxon's inability to give full effect to aspiration.

In the Celtic alphabet there are several letters subjected to aspiration.

B is aspirated Bh equals V in English

C Ch K

D Dh Y

F Fh has no representative sound

G Gh equals Y in English

M Mh V and W

P Ph F

S Sh H

T Th H

It will, from the foregoing table, be seen that the initial consonants of the aspirates are subject to eclipse – that is to say, the aspirate subdues the distinct sound of the primary consonant. The Article *an* plays an important part in the subduing of the aspirates, and is used both before palatals in the masculine sense and before linguals in the feminine sense, as (Mas.) *an cogadh,* the war, *an gniomh,* the deed; (Fern.) *an doimhne mkor,* the great deep, *an nochd,* to-night. The effect ia that in the masculine the initial letter of the word to which it is prefixed is eclipsed as for example *Aber-an-aitionn* – Abernethy; *Camus-an- fhearna – Gamus-nearn.* In the feminine the initial letter of the article is entirely dropped, and the final letter *n* is embodied in the following word as *an-earran* the portion, found as Nearan and Nerrin.

The Norse names can be treated with more certainty being the stratum medium or middle layer, and of more recent date. They retain more of their original appearance and are not subject so largely to elision. The old name of the Lossie River was *Laxa.* The terminal *a* in Norse is river and forms the stem of a great many streams on the continent and elsewhere. The Gothic and old German form is *aha* changed into *au* and *ach,* but the simple *a* or *o* with prefixes expressive of the character of the stream is that used in countries occupied by the Norsemen. It is also very noticeable that wherever the Norse *oe,* o or a are found as distinct from the Anglo-Saxon *ea, ey,* and *ay* an island, these denote the presence of the Vikingr.

The word *Berg* as changed into *Burg* is applied to towns and fortresses, as Burghead. *Bo, Bol,* or *Bolstadr,* a dwelling is widely diffused in the north and west of Scotland as in Skibo, Skelbo, and Embo in Sutherland. It takes the forms of *Busta, Bousta,* and *Bister,* and when used as a generic term, is shortened into *Boat,* which accounts for the number of bosts found in Skye. *Bro* or *Bru,* a . bridge, is found in Brora in Sutherlandshire. *By* or *Bie,* from the Norse verb *biga* to build, is found in the Scotch doric as bigg to build, and as a terminal in Lockerby, Canoby, Canisby and Golspie.

Dai/r, a dale or valley, is usually placed by the Norsemen after the adjective or defining word, as in Laxdale and Swordale, while the Celt adopts the opposite, as in Dallas, Dalness and Dalcross.

Eidh, which looks Celtic, is the Norse for an isthmus, and is found in Ayth and Aith, in Eday and Aisdale, and takes the forms of *ay, eie, vye, uie,* and *eye.*

The Norse *Farr,* a sheep, is found in Sutherland, in Farra, Faray and Fare, a hill in Aberdeenshire. *Feld* or *veld* are not pureNorse, being borrowed from the Teutonic, but *Fell, Fiall,* or *Fjold,* a mountain, are pure Norse, as in Snafel. *Fiord* or *Fjord,* an inlet, takes many forms, as ford, fort, forth, furt, and phonetically *ort, ord, irt,* and *urt.* The Firth of Forth is a tautology. *Fob* or *Fora,* a waterfall, is found in Suyderfors and Forsinard. *Oat,* an opening, is found in Cattegat, Margate, Ramsgate, the passage of Ruim. The word *gat* is cognate with the Indian *ghat,* which is used to signify a passage between hills. *Gill* and *Gja,* a ravine, is found in Ormsgill, Thorsgill named after two of the Norse leaders, and *Almanna-gja Allman's* ravine. The word is cognate with the Hebrew *gae,* also a ravine, and found in Ge-Hinnom. It is met with as *goe,* as in Ravensgoe and Redgoe.

Hafen or *Havn,* a harbour, from *haff,* the ocean, is found in Thorshaven, Stonehaven, Milfordhaven. *Hagen,* an enclosure, is not found in the North of Scotland, but is common on the Continent; but *Hjem,* or *Heim,* cognate with the Greek *keimai,* a home, is quite diffused over the British Isles, and is contracted into *om, um,* and *am;* while *Hel, Helle, Helge,* and *Heil,* prefixes with various meanings, are found scattered throughout the country, generally signifying holy, as in Hellwell the holy well and Heligoland the holy land.

Holm, an island, not common as such, but when used to signify an isolated hill is frequently found. *Hoo* or *Hoe,* a spit of land, are common in the North. The Norse *Kirche,* a church, is certainly the most common of all Norse terms in Scotland; the word is usually derived from the Greek *kuriake,* and many parishes prefix the word as Kirkcaldy, Kirkhill, Kirkconnel. *Lad,* a pile or heap, enters into the names of mountains and high rocks, as *Lad- cragg* and Ladhill, and Leadhills in Lanark. *Lund,* a sacred grove, is found in Lundsgarth and Lundy island.

Mor or *Moer,* waste land or heath, *is* found in all the moors of Scotland; in Scotch it takes the form of Muir. *Noes,* a point or headland, cognate with the Latin *Nasus,* plays an important part in Scotch topography, while equally important is *Nor,* the North. Throughout the Western Isles chiefly we find the word *eyre* or ore *cognate* with Latin *ora,* Greek *horos,* a shore or boundary, as in Airor and Kensaleyre; while *ord,* a point or corner, and *osier,* the east, assert themselves in such places as the Ord in Banff and Ord in Caithness, and Ostend and Osterburg.

Rain, Rand, and *Ra,* a promontory or peninsula, is found in Old Rain, Rhynie, Rhind, Reay.

Scale or *Skali,* a hut or shed from which is taken the Scotch *Sheal* or *Shealing* is very commonly diffused throughout the British Isles, as in Scalloway, Scalby, Galashiels, and Shields, and

Skail in Sutherland.

Skaer, a sharp rock allied to the Welsh *y-sgariad* and Gaelic *Sgeir* is found in Scarnose, Scarabines, and Scordale, while *Skaw* or *Skagi,* an isthmus or promontory, is only found on the continent,

A

and *Stackr,* a projecting rock, is rarely met with in Scotland. *Slav,* a stake, pole, or pillar, and applied to a perpendicular rock, *is* found in Dunstaffnage and Staffa. *Ster,* anciently *setr,* contracted from *stadr,* a station or place, is found in Lybster, Leinster, Munster, and Ulster. *Stor,* great, is found in the Store Rock and Storehammer greathills, and Stoer in Sutherland.,

Taing or *Tanga* a point of land is found in Tongue in Sutherland. *Thing* or *Ting,* a term applied by the Norsemen to their legislative assemblies, and also to places where these assemblies met, is found in Dingwall, Tingwall Tynwald, Tinwald, and Thingwald, and Tain in Ross is the Norse Thing.

Thor and *Thur,* prefixes derived from the Norse god Thor, is

found in Thurso, Thorsoe, and Thorshaven. *Tun,* an enclosure, originally meant a place rudely fortified, and was also applied to farms and manors, and in this sense is still used as *tun* and *toon.*

Vatn or *vand,* a lake, is only found in the western isles, as Vattin in Skye, but *vie, ve, wy,* holy, is found in Advie, Wigan, Wydale, and Wigton.

Voe or *Vogr,* a bay, is found in Laxvoe, Grunavoe, and Westvoe, while *Wick* or *Vig,* a dwelling, village, or town, the primary meaning of which seems to have been a station for ships, but with the Anglo-Saxons a station on land, is one of the most common Norse words round the coast of the British Isles.

These are some of the more common of the important additions made by the Scandinavians and Danes to the place names of Britain, and are easily distinguished because they do not readily lend themselves to assimilation.

In Orkney and Shetland where the sway of the Norsemen obliterated all traces of the Celtic topography, there are only two classes of names – Old Norse and English, and a Norseman of the present day can as easily explicate the place-names there as those who gave the names. In other parts of the country the sway of the Viking was not so long nor so complete, hence a great many of the names have been joined to the names already given, and in the process of transcription have become so obscured that only scholars with a knowledge of both Celtic and Norse can attempt to explicate them. A good example is seen in Kensaleyre – Celtic, *Ceann,* a head ; *Sal,* the sea; and Norse *Eyre* or *Eyrr,* the Shore – The head of the Sea Shore. While we find Norse words conjoined to the original Celtic in many cases, it is not so universal as their conjunction with English, because the two are kindred speeches, consequently Norse names, as might be expectedhave not undergone so many changes. They are still robed, as it were, in their original dress. Even at this remote period of time traces of Norse physiognomy as well as of Norse names are found in the fair-haired, blue-eyed, and round-shouldered men and women found in the north and east of Scotland, to whose progenitors we are indebted for many of the mythologies and customs, traces of which we find in the place names they have left, and which have only been dissipated by the stronger glare of more enlightened times. Their gods and heroes are found in *Thor* and *Ran;* and Harold and Carl and Sweyn, and their usages and customs of measuring land by rentals are found in *penge, penningr,* as in Pennyfeiler, Feorlig, and Unganab.

While there are a few Norse names in Elginshire it is evident that the Norsemen did not, for any length of time, if at all, settle on the southern shores of the Moray Firth, and we have it on the authority of Dr. Skene that Helgi, one of the most notable of the Vikings, whose name had for long been supposed to be found in Elgin, never sailed farther South along the eastern shores of Scotland than the Orkney Islands. The Stone of Sweno in Forres and the Cairn of Duffus are relics pointing out their existence for some time.

The third or upper stratum of names in Elginshire is an intermixture of Ecclesiastical and English names. The former are chiefly attached to the parishes, while the purely English are found attached to modern holdings and reclaimed land.

SECTION 2

THE PLACE NAMES OF ELGINSHIRE.

PARISH OF ABERNETHY.

AT one time this large parish formed a part of the county of Elgin, but some years ago it was put under the jurisdiction of Inverness-shire, although much further removed from the county town than from the county town of Elgin. It is 14 miles in length, 12 in breadth, and is bounded on the south by the famous Cairngorm range of mountains, by the river Spey on the north and west, and by the neighbouring parish of Cromdale on the east. The population is about 1,200. In summer the climate and scenery in this parish are scarcely equalled in all Scotland, and year by year, as this becomes more widely known, many visitors resort thither during the summer season. It is purely a Highland parish, and few if any of its place names indicate the incursions of foreigners who so frequently visited the seaboard of the Moray Firth and left their indelible impression on the places they visited. Nor has the universality of the English language even yet obscured the names given by the first occupants of the soil. Thus the great majority of the names found is as purely Celtic as can be found in

any part of Scotland. There are some words that present difficulties in the way 'of explanation from the fact that they have been already too much explained.

Abernethy is one of these. About Aber, the first part of the word, there has never been any doubt. It is derived from *Ath,* a ford, and *Bior,* water, and is generally supposed to belong to the Welsh rather than to Gaelic, while Inver, meaning the same thing, is the Gaelic form. Aber is chiefly confined to the east of Scotland, while on the west its place is almost entirely occupied by Inver, and means a confluence of waters: here, where the Nethy discharges itself into the Spey. The meaning or origin of the word Nethy has been a topic of discussion for a long time. The common theory is that it is taken from Nechtan, the Pictish king, who is said to have founded a church in Abernethy, Perth, about the year 700. Robertson makes it to come from Neithe, the God of Waters. It is quite plain, however, that he knew not either the spelling or pronunciation of the word, and had written it so as to fit in with his own theory. When it rains very heavy it is quite common in some parts to hear the expression, " Tha na neitheach- ainn a tigheann nuas " – the waters are coming down, or, in other words, the heavens are coming down, showing that Neitheachainn and Neamhain are two words for heavens. In 1292 the form of the word was Nethyn, and we find the same word as the terminal of Cambusnethan in Lanark. The terminal n was dropped about the year 1400. Nethan comes from Aitionn, gorse, broom, or juniper, and Nethyn is from the same root. Aber-n-ationn is doubtless the origin of Abernethy.

Ach-na-gonaln is a combination of the two Gaelic words, *Achadh,* a field or plain, and *Gainailan,* folds or cattle enclosures. *Na* is the genitive form *of,* the field or place of enclosures. Achadhplays an important part in the topography of the country, and is frequently found in the various forms of *Achadh, Auch, Augh,* and *Auchen.* Auchgourish should be *Achadh-gobhairich,* the field of the goats, or goats' pastureland.

Ailen is purely Gaelic without any disguises, and means a green plain or meadow, frequently and perhaps more particularly applied to a green patch in the bottom of a valley.

Aitenlea. Here we have the root *Aitionn,* so often found in this parish, meaning juniper or gorse in combination with lea, or meadow or field, and the word Juniperfield was at one time most applicable.

Dell is not a pure Gaelic word, although the word Dail is commonly used. It is derived from the M. E. dale, Icelandic dalr. In many cases the word Dal means a portion of land or territory as Dalriada, from the Milesian king, Cairbe-Riada.

Tomdow is but slightly different from Tomdubh, the black hillock. We find the word used adjectively in Inchtomach, from the Gaelic *Innis,* a meadow, and *Tomach,* humpy – the humpy meadow

Clachaig. – Clach, a stone, plays an important part in the topography of the country, and the word *Clachan* is frequently met with in Scotland, and was originally employed to define a circle of stones, inside of which the Druidical rites of worship were celebrated, and in course of time churches were erected near these spots, then houses, and thus the application of *Clachan* was extended to mean hamlet, and has now the same meaning as Kirk ton.

Lup-na-damph. – The first part, *Lup,* comes from the Gaelic *Lub,* a bend or incline or elbow of a hill. *Na* is the genitive form *of,* and the latter part is from *Damh,* an ox, and when applied inhigh land, frequently meaning a stag, as probably in this case – the ox or deer pastureland.

Glenlochy. – In Adamnan's Life of Columba the word *Lochy* is written *Lochdiae,* a Latinised form of Lochdubh, the black loch, but probably the word Lochy here means the little loch – Glenlochy, the glen of the little loch.

Garten, a tilled piece of ground, sometimes *Goirtean,* is derived from the Teutonic *Garth* or *Gart,* and in Ireland is found in the form of *Gort.* The Welsh is *Garrd* or *Garz.* It is also applied to an enclosed place, as a stackyard or a fold for cattle.

Banedden. – This word comes from *Bun,* literally a root, but here meaning the mouth, and *Feadan,* a small stream. *Bun* is frequently met with in Scotland, as in Bunowen, the mouth of the Avon; Bunawe, at Lochawe; and Buness, the mouth of the cascade.

Lairg is taken from the Gaelic Learg, a slope, and is found in Sutherland as Lairg, in Ayr as Largs, in Fife as Largo, and there is Largan-na-greana, the sunny slope, and Largan-reagh, the smooth slope.

Muckrach. – Sir Herbert Maxwell makes this word to mean swine pastureland. Although the wild boar was common in the country in days long ago, it is very doubtful whether the application is correct. There is another word *Muerach,* literally meaning a sand hillock, but generally applied to undulating, uneven, ground, which is evidently the signification here.

Druim is the Gaelic for a ridge, from *Drama,* the backbone of an animal, cognate with Latin *Dorsum,* and is met with in the various forms of *Dram, Drum, Drym, Dreem,* conspicuously found in Drumalban or Dorsum Britanniae.

Cullachie. – The first part, *Cull,* must not be confounded with*Cul,* a corner. It is from *Coille,* wood, and *Achadh,* a field – the woodland stretch. *Coille* is found in this form in Culleen, a little wood, and Barnacullia, the top of the wood.

Rynattin, from the Gaelic *Reidh,* a plain, and *Aitionn,* juniper. The Welsh form of the word is *Eithin,* and prominent in the topography of Scotland.

Garline is from the Gaelic *Garbh;* Welsh, *Garw,* rough; and *Lian,* a field – the rough field or marsh. *Lianaig* is a small field.

Tulloch, from *Tulach,* a hill, and sometimes a measure of land, and variously found as *Tulla, Tullow, Tully,* and *Tulli.* It is, however, more frequently used in the adjectival form than as a substantive.

Delbog. – The prefix *Del* is defined above; *Bog* comes from the Gaelic *Bog,* wet or marshy – the marshy dell.

Congash is an expressive word from the two Gaelic words *Con,* equal to the English *co,* as in co-operate, and *Gats,* a torrent. Congash is the confluence of two streams.

Pit-youlish. – *Pit* or *Pitten,* a hollow, is an old Pictish word, with which is cognate the Anglo-Saxon Pyt, Latin Puteus, a well. In the Book of Deer it is found as *Pette,* where the meaning of *Baile,* a town or dwelling-place, is attached to it, and in many places it is now made the substitute for *both,* old Gaelic form *Buth,* with which is cognate the Icelandic *Bud,* Swedish *Bod,* allied to the Sanskrit *Bha-yana,* a house, from the root word *Bhu.* That *Pit* is interchangeable with *both* can be seen from Pitgavenie, formerly *Bothgounan,* the smith's dwelling, made historically famous by Shakespeare as the scene of Macbeth's assassination of Duncan, and from Pitcairn, formerly Bothcarn. In 1667 the word was *Pit-ghouish.* From this it is easy to arrive at the proper meaning, which is Pit-a-ghiuthais, the firwood hollow.

Ellan-eorn. – *Ailean* is a fertile piece of ground, and *Eorna* is the Gaelic for barley. Barley being a surface feeding cereal, shallow humic soil is more suitable for growing it, and as a consequence many patches of such soil are called *Ailean-eorna.*

Coul-na-fea. – The first part, *Coul,* is from *Cnil,* a moor or hollow, and *Fea* comes from the Gaelic *Feidh,* deer – the deer's hollow or the deer's retreat.

Lyne-beg, from the Welsh *Llyn,* Gaelic *Linn,* a pool, with which is cognate the Anglo-Saxon *Hlynna,* and *Beg,* little – Linn bheag, the little stream.

Connege. – In 1690 *Conait* is an old Gaelic word meaning a stream, as *Conait* in Perth and *Conan* in Ross.

Auchernack is an unpardonable corruption from *Achadh- f/uarnach,* meaning the field of the alderwood.

Duack is the hard form of *Duag,* black water. In this and the foregoing word the substitution of the hard terminals for the soft would indicate at some time the influence of the Norse elements.

Rye-hillock – from the two Gaelic words *Reidh,* a stretch of land, and *Seileach,* the willow – the willow field or plain.

Ault-garroch – from the Gaelic Allt, a stream or burn, and *Garbhach* or *Garroch,* turbulent – the turbulent stream.

Bail-an-tya – from the Gaelic Baile, a residence, town, or hamlet, and Tuath, tenantry, here probably meaning a community. *Leitir-aiten* – from the Gaelic *Leitir,* the side of a hill, and *Aitionn,* gorse or broom, literally meaning Broomhill.

Auld-charn – from the Gaelic *Allt,* a burn or stream, and *Cam* or Cairn, a pile of stones, here probably meaning a rock. The cairns are frequently met with throughout the North of Scotland, and were first of all erected to mark the spots where the couriers who carried the fiery cross were to meet.

Coul-na-Kyle. – This is a mutilated form of the Gaelic words *Cuil-na-Coille,* the woody hollow, or the woody back of a hill. The word *Coille* is met with in various forms throughout the country. Kel, Kil, Kelly, Killy, and Kyle. The Cymric form of the word is *Coed* or *Coid,* variously written as *Cuit, Coat,* and *Cuit,* a wood.

Slia-more. – The first part, *Slia,* is from the Gaelic *Sliabh,* a mountain or heath, and is found as *Slieve* or *Slieu,* akin to the German *Sliet,* a declivity. The latter part, More, is from the Gaelic *Mor,* large – the great hill.

Tober-aie. – In 1G70 it was Tobar-fhaidh, which is the literal Gaelic for the seer's or prophet's well. *Tobar* is from the Pictish *Dobhair,* water, and *Faidh* is a prophet or seer. "Wells were held in great veneration by the Celts in heathen times," both in Scotland and Ireland, and upon the introduction of Christianity by St. Columba many of his followers erected their churches near these venerated wells, which were called after the particular saint, by which they are known to this day. Some wells were supposed to be possessed of certain charms or healing virtues. *Tobar-nam-buadh* in Skye is the well of virtues, and the rivers *Tiber* in Italy and the *Tiveront* (Tobar-abhuinn) are from the same root.

Ballintuim is from Baile, a dwelling, and *Tom,* a hillock or rising ground. The dwelling on the hill.

Lyn-a-chail. – Lyn here does not mean a pool of water, but is derived from, or is rather the Anglicised form of, an old Gaelic word, *Lann,* a piece of enclosed ground or garden, and variously found as *Lyn, Lynn,* and *Lin,* which are the oblique forms of *Lainn. Chail* is from the Gaelic Cal, cabbage. *Lyn-a-chail* is the cabbage garden.

Upper and Nether *Plotta.* At first sight *Plotta* would seem to be a Norse word, *Flatr,* or Danish *Flada,* a flat isle. It is not so, but is from the Gaelic *Pladain,* a plot of ground. The upper and lower plots of ground.

Tombae – from the two Gaelic words *Tom,* a hillock, and *Beithe,* birchwood – the birchwood hill.

Buck-charn, in 1670 Buck-arn – from middle English *Bukke,* Anglo-Saxon *Bucca,* a he goat, Dutch *Bok,* Icelandic *Bukkr,* Swedish *Bock,* Danish *Buk,* German *Bock,* Gaelic and Irish *Boc,* and Sanskrit *Bukka.* The name would seem to be applied to a mountain here, and *Am,* a place which eagles frequent, as Amis- dale and Knock-arn, the eagles' mountain.

Lyne-breck. – *Lyne* here means a pool, and *Breac,* trout – the trout's pool.

Ellan is another form of the word *Ailean,* a green plain or meadow, very common in the country.

Ballifurth. – In 1600 it was *Balifert. Baile,* the first part, is one of the most prevalent of prefixes in Scottish topography. *Pert,* the latter, is almost now an obsolete word in Gaelic, although still common in Irish. It signifies a grave or trench, and is found as a prefix in the term *Feart-thuinn,* rain, or a place for holding water.

Topper-fettle – from the Gaelic *Tobar,* a well, and *Feadail,* cattle; also *Feudail.* Italy, anciently *Eudalia,* conies from this word, and signifies the country adapted for rearing cattle. Topper- fettle means the cattle's drinking place or well.

Mullingarroch. – Before the days of steam the meal or grinding mills were erected on the banks of rivers and streams with sufficient supply of water. *Mullin* is the Gaelic for mill, and *Garroch,* from Garbh, rough or turbulent, and *Ach,* the Norse water – the mill on the turbulent stream.

Braeniddin. – The first part is from the Gaelic *Braigh,* a top orsummit, and frequently an incline. Brae is the Scotch form, and is found as *Bri, Bre,* and *Bray.* The is a contraction of *an,* the genitive preposition *of; Iddin* is a corruption of *Aodann,* a face, and is found as *Edin, A din, Odin, Eden.* The word signifies brae face.

Rynirich – from the Gaelic *Reidh,* a plain or slope, and *Feurach,* grassy – the grassy slope.

Cichauloope, in 1722 *Cioch-an-luib.* – The first part, *doch,* has the same meaning as the word Pap, in the Pap of Caithness, and signifies an isolated knoll, and *Luib* is a bend – the knoll at the apex of the bend.

Rynuan – from the Gaelic *Reidh,* a plain or slope, and *Uafi,* a lamb – the sheep's slope or hill.

Doir – from the Gaelic *Doire,* a grove, a thicket, or an insulated clump of trees.

Ry-voan, Gaelic *Reidh,* a plain, and *Mhoine,* peaty or mossy – the mossy plain.

K t KV *f*

Ryncleich, in 1700 *Reidh-na-cloich,* stony field.

Causor. – There is a Gaelic word *Casair,* signifying phosphorescent light proceeding from old wood in the dark, and what is commonly called by Gaelic-speaking people *Teine-sionnachan.* The same word is also differently applied to mean a thorn, slaughter, carnage, and probably the latter is the proper signification.

Corchully – from the Gaelic *Coire,* a deep gully or mountain dell, and *Coille,* wood – the woody mountain dell.

Lurg – from the Gaelic *Learg,* a slope or hillside, as found in Lairg in Sutherland, Largs, and Largo.

BaInagowan, G&ec Baile-na-gobhainiiQ smith's dwelling-place.

Lynstock – from *Linn,* a pool and *Stnchd,* allied to the Norse, *Stalk,* a cliff making a cascade – the cascade pool.

Sliachlach – from the Gaelic *Sliabh,* a hill, and *Clach* or *Clachach,* rocky – the rocky mountain.

I ; I

. !" *Derrydow* – from the Gaelic *Doire,* a grove or thicket, or hollow,

and *Dubh,* black or dark – the dark or shady hollow. *p Lanntichan.* – The first part *Lann,* of this word is a root common to several languages. In middle English it was *Laind,* with the d dropped; in old French it was *Lande,* Spanish *Landa,* a wild, untilled, shrubby, or grassy plain; Welsh *Llan,* and Gaelic *Laun ;* English *Lawn.* Its primary meaning seems to be an enclosed piece of ground. It is not found extensively in local nomenclature. *Tichan,* the latter part, comes from *Tiadhan,* , a little hill. The word signifies the hill enclosure. *Lann* has afterwards come to mean a church, from the fact that it was usually built in an enclosed piece of ground.

Croft-na-queen. – This word has assumed an English form. So late as 1798 it was *Croit-na-cuinne,* the corner croft.

Croft-ronan was in the same year *Croit-Ronan* – the croft of St. Ronan. This, however, is doubtful, as St. Ronan died in the year 737 in the island of North Rona, but probably his followers might have named the place after him, as many other places in Scotland have been so named.

Croft-na-haven was *Croft-na-hamhuinn* – the croft on the bank of a stream or river.

Anadorach. – The first part is a contraction of *Amhuinn,* a river, and *Dorrach* is the Gaelic for rough or turbulent – the rough flowing stream.

Tonterrie in 1790 was *Tonntir,* from the Gaelic *Tonn,* a wave or undulation, and *Tir,* the land, cognate with the Latin *Terra* – the undulating land.

Lettoch. – The word *Davach* is frequently met with in the place

names of the north-east of Scotland, and means a measure of land. Originally it was a measure of capacity, and the extent of land that would take a davach of corn to sow it was itself called Davach. The half of that extent was a half davach, or in Gaelic *leth-dabhach* or lettoch.

Revach – from the Gaelic *Reidh,* a plain or slope, and *Bac/td,* the summit – the summit plain.

Curr, a Gaelic word meaning a corner, an end, a pit, a fountain, and situation or site, and is frequently met with in topography.

Lyne-cork – from *Lann,* an enclosed piece of ground; *Corca,* oats – a piece of enclosed ground suitable for growing oats.

Inch-brock – from the Gaelic *Innis,* pasture-land near water, and the Gaelic word for badger is *Broc,* which is usually Anglicised *Brock,* and found in the terminals *brock,* na-brock, nam-brock, of the badgers, and *brocach* means the haunts of the badgers, while *Brocair* is the badger or fox hunter.

Tomchrocher. – Tom is a hill or knoll, and Crocher is from the Gaelic *Crochaire,* a villain, one deserving to be hanged, from which we have another substantive, *Crochadair,* a hangman. *Tomeroc/ier* is the villain's or hangman's hill, the latter probably, as in olden times executions usually took place on some high ground.

Rynerick – from the Gaelic *Reidh,* a plain, and *Eirig,* a ransom, forfeit, reparation, amercement, or fine – a piece of good forfeited land.

Achgourish – from the Gaelic *Achadh,* a field, and *lubhar,* or *Iubharach,* the yew tree – the field of the yew wood.

3

SECTION 3

II.

THE PARISH OF ALVES.

THIS parish lies in the North-West of Elginshire. It includes about a mile of coast, and is 6J miles long and 5$ miles broad. Its area is about 9404 square acres, valuation about $9000, and population a little over 1000. The surface presents a pleasant diversity of hill and dale and undulating ground. The land here shows evidence of early cultivation, and in several places historical remains of the long past have been unearthed in fields where the plough has been at work for ages. Some years ago a cist constructed of rude stone slabs jointed together with something like bitumen was discovered on the farm of Wester Alves, containing what appeared to be the bones, not well preserved, of a female. In one of the jawbones handled there were several teeth, on two of which the enamel was pretty well preserved. This discovery led to the belief that others might be got in the neighbourhood, but as no extensive excavations were made since, none has been found. The knock on the eastern boundary of the parish is crowned by a tower, from which an extensive view of the surrounding country and of Ross and Sutherland across the Moray Firth can be commanded. By tradition the knock is connected with the story of Macbeth and the witches. Possibly there may be some foundation for this, as the knock is on the road between Bothgownan and the

Blasted Heath, the one by a curiouscoincidence being about three miles east of Elgin, and the other a similar distance east of Nairn.

But the object (here) is not to write the history of Moray, but to show that the topographical names of the county are of considerable historical interest and importance, and to show that from these names, although the Gael was the native occupant of the soil, the seaboard districts of the county frequently made the acquaintanceship of Danes and Scandinavians, who crossed the German Ocean on their marauding expeditions.

Taking the parishes in alphabetical order, we have first the Parish of Alves. The configuration of this parish and its place names go a long way to suggest that at some remote period of the country's history there was a large river flowing eastward through the low ground between the parishes of Alves and Duffus, very likely the Findhorn, or *Eren,* as it was anciently called, and forming one *outtum fluminis* with the *Laxia* and *Spechan* – the Lossie and Spey. The word Alves itself furnishes a good example. It is derived, the first part, from *Abh,* water, which is allied to the Sanskrit *ahab,* as in Douab, Chenab, in India; to the Norse *aa,* as in Lena, sluggish river; Laxa, salmon river; Thurso, Thor's river. *Ess,* the latter part, is simply the Gaelic *Eas* a stream. In Celtic countries *Abh* is frequently applied to a ford. It should be remembered that in *Abh* the aspirates bh equal v. Alves, therefore, means *Abh-eas,* the ford of the river.

Another example is *Inchstellie,* Gaelic *innis,* an island, and very frequently pastureland near water, with which is cognate the Welsh *ynys,* German *insel,* Latin *insula,* and Greek *nesos. Stellie,* the latter part of the word, comes from the Teutonic *stal, stuhl,* and *stelle,* a place, seat, or farm. Inchstellie, the island farm, or the pastureland farm.

The next word, *Ordies,* supplies, evidence of the irregular action of water, from the Norse *ord,* Dutch *oort,* and German *ort,* a point, a corner, or a round knoll. The terminal diminutive here strongly suggests that the word Ordies means undulating ground or little knolls. Then comes *Carsewell.* The first part, *Carse,* of this word is generally thought to be from the Scotch, while as a matter of fact it is from *cars,* a word peculiar to the Armoric dialect of the Celtic, and meaning a level, fertile tract of country. The word *well* is a superimposed addition to denote a spring of water in the carse.

Earnside. Eren was the ancient name of the Findhorn, from which doubtless the form *Earn* is taken. A considerable difference of opinion has for a long time prevailed regarding the derivation of this word. Dr. Skene says it is derived from *Eire,* the Irish Queen mentioned in Nennius, who is supposed to have gone from Scotland. Windisch, another eminent writer, gives it as from the Gaelic *earruinn,* & fertile portion of land. Rhys puts it far back into the pre-Celtic period, a fashion of his with words he cannot explain. He has not told us yet when the pre-Celtic period ended and the Celtic period began, and Robertson makes it to be composed of two words, *"Ear,"* the east, and *"An,"* a contraction of *abliuinn,* a river – the east-flowing river. The Earn in Perth was formerly called *Eirenn,* which is a near approximation to Eren. We find the same word disguised in Nairn, anciently Inver-na-ruinn. It does not follow that because all these forms have a certain semblance they are correct Our ancestors did not go about the nomenclature of the country without palpable objects in view. Dr. Skene "s derivation cannot therefore be accepted, because he has gone on the assumption that all the Earns in Scotland havethe same improbable origin. Robertson's derivation is purely fanciful, while Windisch's meaning, though nearer the point, is still not correct. When it is considered that the valleys and straths through which these rivers flow are rich, fertile pieces of land, there is a good deal to be said for his meaning. There is an old Pictish word, Earran, modern Gaelic, Earrann, meaning an end, limit, extremity, a water boundary. This is the origin of the word Earn, and upon investigation it will be found that every Earn in Scotland at one time formed the specific boundary of a particular district, hence Earn means Earran, the boundary river.

The word *Cloves* is of more recent origin, and indicates the presence of the Norsemen in the country. It is derived from the Danish *Klove,* a hollow at the foot of a slope, and cognate with it are the Anglo-Saxon *Cleofan,* Dutch *Kloven,* Icelandic *Kljufa,* and German *Kliben,* Gaelic *Clu,* a sheltered spot. *Monaughty is* a pure Gaelic word from *Monadh,* a moorish hill, and frequently contracted into *Mon* and *Man. Aughty* is from *Aite,* a place of residence, which in this case means the hill farm.

Reeves is another impression from the Norsemen. It is taken from the Icelandic *Greifi,* a steward or governor, here meaning the steward's portion or possibly the factor's farm. *Lachlan-wells,* formerly *Lochlin,* without the *wells.* Lochlin is a Gaelic substantive meaning hollow, and it is to this day applied to Holland, and a Dutchman is always called a Lochlineach. *Cardonhill,* anciently *Caerdun,* indicates the presence of the Cymric element in the North. It comes from the Welsh *Caer,* a fort, and *Dun,* a hill . It is probable this name was given by monks of the order of St. Asaph in Wales, who are said to have been in Morayshire. We find the same word slightly different inGarden in Peebles, Cardon-ness in Kirkcudbright, and Cardowan in Lanarkshire.

Wards. – This word is pretty common along the north-east coast of Scotland wherever the Norsemen landed. Besides this one we find the name in Cruden (Aberdeen), Caithness, and Orkney. It is derived from the Norse *Wart, Warth,* and means a tower or beacon; Anglo-Saxon *Wardian,* German *Warten,* to guard. Then there is *Waring,* a fortification. *Asliesk,* an old ruined tower in the parish, situated on the side of a ridge. The word is a combination of the Norse and Gaelic – *As* or *Aas,* Norse, a hill ridge; and *Slios,* Gaelic, the side of the ridge. *Toreduff* is a native word, from the Gaelic *Torr,* a conical hill, cognate with which are the Welsh *Twr,* French *Tur,* Latin *Turris,* and Greek *Pyrgos.* The latter part, Duff, comes from the Gaelic *Dubh,* black. The name black hill was once very applicable. Hempriggs (in Elgin and Caithness) is derived from the Anglo-Saxon *Henep,* signifying hemp. This word was borrowed at an early period from the Latin *Cannabis,* Greek *Kannabis,* and has undergone many consonantal letter changes. We have the Dutch *Hennep,* from which source we probably got it in Scotland, Icelandic *Hampr,* Danish *Hamp,* all meaning the plant hemp. *Riggs,* the latter part of the word, comes from Icelandic *Hryggr,* literally a ridge, but commonly used in such expressions as a ploughed rig. Hempriggs means patches of land for growing hemp. Muirhead. – The word Muir is quite common throughout Scotland, so much so that many people look upon it as an indigenous word. We are, however, indebted to our Danish invaders for its introduction. Danish *Moer,* a moor or swamp, or a mossy plateau, as the moor of Rannoch.

Moray s-Cairn. – The derivation of the name Moray has longMoray.

been a source of considerable speculation among philologists. Sir Herbert Maxwell, the latest writer on the subject, says it is derived from the two Gaelic words *Alur,* the sea, and *Magh,* a plain or land, and makes it to mean the land overlooking the sea. He arrives at this conclusion by taking an old spelling or form, *Mureff.* Then he takes *Magh,* and eliminates the double consonantal aspirate (gh), for which he substitutes the double (f). He also banishes the initial letter M, and appends the *effio Mur,* and thus arrives at *Mureff.* If this were the oldest form of the word there might be some ground for the meaning, but in the year 970 the Pictish chronicle gives it as *Morovia,* in 1085 we have *Murieh,* in 1200 *Mureff,* and in 1295 *Morref.* So that the form Sir Herbert has adopted is rather a late one. There is little doubt that the form *Morovia* in the Pictish Chronicle is nearest to that in which it was left by the Romans, and as they as a rule did not give new names, but only Latinised those they found, *Morovia* is therefore nearer the original, which ought to be taken into account in the explication of the word. If we could only strip these Roman disguises from the words there would be little trouble in finding the original form. It will be observed that in the first part of the word as given in the various forms there is little change, with the exception of the alternate transposition of the vowels *o* and ; that is to say, making the first syllable at one time *Mor,* at another *Mur,* the first signifying large or big, the latter signifying the sea. It is therefore a question which of these is the one really meant. If it were *Mur,* the sea, it would have been easy for the Romans to have used their own word *Mare* without disguising the meaning, but being *Mor,* they left it as they found it. It is a violation of Gaelic idiom to prefix *Mur* to *Magh,* because it only conveys a general and not an applicable expressionof " land overlooking the sea." Retaining the first adjectival form *Mor,* big, and affixing thereto the Gaelic *Aibh,* the plural form of *Abh,* a river, we have the word *Moraibh,* pronounced *Moraine,* signifying the district of large rivers. The ancient province of Moray extended from Petri-Promontorium in the east to Varar on the west, a stretch of country through which more than any other in Scotland there flows a large number of rivers. The two districts, Morava and Moravia, on the Continent, signify river districts.

The next word, *Ardgye,* is derived from the Gaelic *Ardgaoith,* the windy height, and is a common name in the country. The final *th* is frequently dropped, and we find it variously spelled *gey, gie, gye, gee, gi.*

Ryeyards at first sight appears to be purely English. It was formerly *Rathard,* from the Gaelic *Rath,* a round earthen fort, a mound, and often a hill, and *Ard,* a height. *Cothill* is locally supposed to be the hill of the Cots. This, however, is too recent a meaning. It comes from the Welsh *Coed,* a wood, and variously written *Coit, Cot, Coat,* and *Cuit,* as found in Cotswold hills, woody hills; *Coitmore,* the big wood; *Glascoed,* greenwood; *Cal-de-cot,* corrupt from Cit-y-Coed, the woody retreat; and *Caleots,* also the woody retreat. This word *Coed,* a wood, though found in place names, is more a Welsh word, while *Coille* is more frequently used in Scotland, as found in the next word, *Coltficld,* which has also the appearance at first sight of being purely English. It was formerly written *Cuiltfield,* from *Coillte,* the plural of *Coille,* wood, and *Veld,* a hill.

Brodieshitt, formerly *Brothichill* We find this same word in *Aber-brothoc,* and means a marsh, the hill beside the marsh.

Crook of Alves. – The word *Crook* is taken from the Icelandic*Krockr,* Swedish *Krok,* which indicates the presence of the Norsemen.

Kilnfiat, formerly *Kilfleot,* from the Gaelic *Kil,* a cell or church, and the Dutch *Vliet,* a channel or arm of the sea – the church by the water.

Clachbrae comes from *Clach,* a stone, and *Brae,* an incline – the stoney brae.

4

SECTION 4

III.

PARISH OF BELLIE.

THIS parish is situated on the east side of the Spey. Its length is nearly six miles, breadth about four miles, with an area of 13,212 acres, for the most part allotted into large farms. The valuation is about $11,000, and the population 4500. At one time the greater part of the parish was attached to the county of Banff, but some years ago a readjustment was made by which the whole was put under the jurisdiction of Elginshire. The Romans, in their circumnavigation round Britain at the beginning of the Christian era, are said to have landed at the mouth of the Spey in this parish, and made an encampment there, vestiges of which are said to be still visible. In Ptolemy's Geography the river Spey is called Teussis, from the Greek word Teukrion, the technical term for the common plant spleenwort, frequently met with on the banks of the river. As a rule the names in the Parish of Bellie do not belong to the Norse element; wherever the names abound in prefixes it may be safely concluded they are of native origin. Celtic names abound in superimposed additions, and frequent reduplications or tautological names are found.

Bellie itself is one of the former. Etymologists have given various derivations of the word. One has it from the Gaelic*Bealaidh* – broom, another that it comes from *Baile,* a town, village, or house, another that it is from the corrupt word *Bel,* a ford. All these are only euphonical guesses without regard to circumstances or the conftguration of the place. The real signification of the word is from the two Gaelic words, *Beal,* the mouth, and *Abh,* a river – the mouth of the river Spey. This is also in keeping with the names given to all the other places at the mouths of rivers along the Moray Firth. Banff, from *Bunabh* – the river mouth; Forres, from *For* and *Eas* – land at the ess or river; Inverness – the mouth of the river; and Beauly, so often attributed to the French Beau-lieu, is nothing else than Bellie, or *Beal-abh,* over again. Our progenitors paid a great deal more respect to system and method in the process of land naming than they get credit for in the present age. Wherefore we must be careful in, as far as possible, finding out their design or reason for giving the particular name.

Dallachy is a combination of two Gaelic words with a reduplicated or tautological meaning, and is derived from *Dail,* a field or valley, and akin to the Welsh *Dol,* Scandinavian *Dahl,* German *Thai,* and *Achadh,* also a field – literally the plain of the field.

Carse-moor. – How two words so antagonistic in signification as *Carse,* from the Armoric dialect of the Celtic *Cars,* a fertile tract of land; and the Norse *Moer,* waste land or heath, should be combined together is explained by the fact that the name was originally given to a large level tract of heath.

Tynet, in 1667 *Tinait* – from the two Gaelic words *Tigh* (sounded *ti),* a house, and *Aite,* a place or site – the sight of the house or dwelling.

Bogmoor, in 1686 *Bogmore* – from the Gaelic *Bog* and sometimes *Bnige,* a marsh, and *Mor,* big or large – the greatmarsh. From the root Bog we have the Gaelic Bogan and Boganach, Irish Bogach – a quagmire.

Cowiemoor, in 1667 *Cobha-more* – from the Gaelic word *Cobhar,* literally foam or froth, and frequently applied to marshy places, and especially to quagmires, and Mor, as in the foregoing word Bogmoor.

Sauchwells is directly derived from the Scotch *Sauch.* Old English *Salig, Salh;* Latin *Salix,* and Gaelic *Saileach,* the willow, and is met with in such words as Sauchieburn and Sauchrie, meaning the willow burn and the willow field.

Cunnen-haugh. – Celtic people seem to have in some way associated the rabbit with *Cu,* the dog or hound, of which the word *Coinen* is a diminutive and is the Gaelic for rabbit. It is akin to the Danish *Kanin,* Scandinavian *Kannina,* Latin *Cunicnlus,* and the English *Coney.* Haugh in Scotland denotes a low-lying meadow between hills or on the banks of a river. Thus the word means the *Coinen-haugh* or the rabbit warren.

Long-howe, in 1674 *Loh-howe.* – Taking the earlier form, evidently the prefix here is a foreign word. Dutch *Loh, Loo, Loke,* a meadow, prefixed to the middle English *Heigh, Hey, Hy ;* Anglo-Saxon *Heah, Heh ;* Dutch *Hoog;* Icelandic *Har;* German *Hawks, Hocks,* a hill or long stretch of hillside – the hill pasture.

Auch-in-reath – from the Gaelic *Achadh,* a field, and *Reidh,* smooth or plain, free from undulations – the smooth or level field.

Ordifish, in 1667 *Ord-a-gonsh.* – Ord is from the Scandinavian *Ord,* Dutch *Oort,* and German *Ort,* a point, a corner, elbow of a hill, and sometimes a place. *Goush* is evidently the Gaelic *Giuthas,* fir – the firwood hill. The name is found in the beginning of the century as Ordiquish.

Floods is not a common word in the northern part of Scotland. It is of Teutonic origin – *Fleot, Fliez,* Dutch *Wleit,* Gaelic *Fleod,* or *Fleod-radh,* literally signifying floating, a flush of water, but more frequently applied to a narrow channel or arm of the sea, as found in the river *Fleet,* Loch *Fleet.* We have it also as *Floss,* as in the Mill on the Floss, and akin to *Adflumina,* at the stream.

Auld-thash. – The prefix here is from the Gaelic *Allt,* a burn Anciently the word was *Ault-gash.* The latter part is an old form of Giuthas, the firwood burn.

Byres, in 1542 *Bairs ;* 1660 *Byrys.* – Taking the earlier form approximating the original, the word is derived from the Gaelic *Bair,* a battle, strife, rout. The supposition is general that between the natives and the Danes a struggle had taken place here. Old people still call the place *Ma-bhar,* from *Magh,* a plain, and *Bair,* the battlefield.

Ault-derg is derived from the two Gaelic words *Allt,* a burn, and *Dearg,* red, which affix is frequently found in the place names of Scotland as in Benderg. *Ruadh* is another word for red, and is also frequently used in topography – *Cnocan-ruadh,* the red hill.

Delfur. – The first part of this word is from the Gaelic *Dail,* a plain or field. *Fur* is from *Fuar,* signifying cold, and is found as part of a great many names, the place so designated being probably exposed to the north, or being marshy, cold spots. The word *Fuar* is as frequently found as a prefix to the noun which it qualifies, as in *Forgie,* where the adjective *Fuar* acts as a prefix. The latter part of the word is from *Gaoth,* wind, and is representative of exposed, bleak situations, which are often designated by the word Forgie, the windy land or windy place.

Shiel is one of the few Norse words found in this parish, *Skali,* Icelandic *Skjol,* Swedish *Skjul,* literally a temporary summer hut. The word used in this country is *Slteiling,* in Ireland *Sheelin,* and used in the hills in the days of summer herding.

Starry-haugh. – The first part of this word is a Low German root, *Ster,* or *Ester,* a stream, and must not be confounded with the Scandinavian *Ster* or *Stadr,* a station or place. Forestman eays that in Germany he finds more than a hundred streams with the root *Sir,* and we find the same root in this country in such streams as the *Stour,* the *Ister.* It is very common all over the Continent. *Haugh* is from the Scotch *Hengh,* and is found in *How* and *Hope,* and generally denotes a low-lying meadow on the banks of a stream. The word signifies the haugh stream.

Chapclford, from the Celtic *Capel,* German *Kapelle,* both of which are probably derived from the Latin *Capella,* a chapel or small church, and the Anglo-Saxon *Ford,* German *Furt* or *Furth,* Dutch *Foord,* a shallow passage over a river, and is frequently found in placenames, as in Coil-an-togle ford in Scott's " Lady of the Lake."

Culriach, from the two Gaelic words, *Cul* or *Cuil,* a nook or corner, and often, at the back of the land. The second part, *Riach,* is from *Riabhach,* greyish, brindled, or grizzled. This particular place was once covered over with the plant louse-wort, and the Gaelic name for it is *Riabhach,* having got the name from its greyish appearance, which makes the word to mean the louse-wort corner.

Wellheads. – The prefix of this name is not, as might at first sight be supposed, from the Anglo-Saxon Well, but from the German *Wila,* a hamlet. It is often met with in the North of Scotland, as in Langwell and Braelangwell in Ross, Kintradwell in Sutherland.

Dryburn. – The prefix *Dry* in this word does not signify theabsence of water. In olden times and in some remote places at the present time illicit stills had been erected in secluded places where good water could be easily obtained. Such was once the case beside this burn. The Gaelic for malt is *Drabh,* English *draff,* and the old form of the word is *Dra-bnrn.*

Ryeriggs. – The first part is from the Gaelic *Reidh,* a smooth, level field, and old English *Hriek,* Icelandic *Hryggr,* Danish *Ryg,* a ridge of land – the smooth riggs.

Auchinhalrig, – Here we have a Celtic word as a prefix to a Norse word – *Achadh,* a field, *na, of,* and *halr,* a slope – the field of the hillside slope. The Danish *Ryg,* a ridge of land, forms the appendix.

Braes is from an old Norse word *Bra,* a hill slope, and cognate with the Gaelic *Braigh,* signifying the top of the hill. It is met with in Braehead, in Bracmar, Braes in Skye and Shetland

Fochabers. – In the year 1125, when the Priory of Urquhart was founded by David I. of Scotland, Fochabers was then called the Village of *Fothopir,* after the Thane of Fothopir, who was superior. This form of the word continued down till about 1325, when it was *Fouchabre,* in 1514 it was *Fochabars,* in 1660 it was *Fochabar,* and about the middle of last century it assumed its present form. If the earlier form be taken, the signification of the word is very different from what it is generally supposed to be, and as anciently, according to the late Professor Blackie, it was *Beulath,* there are reasonable grounds to suppose that Fothopir was the original form of the present name. *Foth* is a Pictish word signifying land, as found in Fotheringham and Foveran; *Opir* is the Pictish form of the present Gaelic word Abar or Eabar, a marsh, bog, or fen, a large tract of marshy ground. Thus the word would mean the marshy land, which is not at all inconsistent with the nature of the ground*as* it would likely be in those early days. The signification usually given is from the Gaelic *Faich,* also a field or plain, and allied to *Foth* and *Aber,* the mouth of a river – the plain at the mouth of the river. Looking at the word as it was in 1514 and 1660, the forms of *Abers* and *Abliar* seem to support the idea of the place being a marsh or fen, and the situation of the town is six miles from the mouth of the river.

5

SECTION 5

IV.

PARISH OF BIRNIE.

THE parish of Birnie lies south of Elgin, which bounds it on the east, north, and west. It is bounded on the south by Rothes and Dallas. It is the most sparsely peopled parish in the county. In the year 667 the valuation was $734 13s. 8d.; nearly one hundred years after it was twopence less, $734 13s. 6d, and now it is about $3000.

Birnie has long been known as one of the earliest spots in Scotland where the Christian faith had been established, and it is now universally thought, as stated by Dr. Cameron Lees in his history of Inverness, that St. Columba himself erected the first church there, from which as a base of their missionary operations his missionaries made pilgrimages throughout the north and east of Scotland. The earliest form of the name Birnie is *Brinuth,* as given in the latter part of the tenth century. Celtic ecclesiastical names are the most complex and puzzling of all land names. Many of the old saints are to us very dim personages, only legendary beings at best, whose history and identity it is at this remote period of time, particularly in the absence of documentary evidence, almost impossible to establish with any degree of certainty. In topography, however, it is remarkable that while church names are very common on the west of Scotland, secular names have as a rule been retained on the east of

Scotland, with few exceptions, such as Birnie, Lumphannan, Tannadyce, and Brechin. The fact that this parish is one of the exceptions is in itself powerful evidence of its early occupation as a missionary station. St. Brendan, the titular saint, was the friend and contemporary of St. Columba, and the old kirk of Birnie must have been built on the site of the old Cathedral of Birnie founded by St. Brendan. In 1200 we meet with the name as Brennach. The Irish for Brendan is Brennach, while the Gaelic is Brennan. In either the Irish or Gaelic form the word means the portion of St. Brendan, in exactly the same sense as Kirrimuir means the big quarter or portion given to the bishop, and Brechin means the portion of St. Bricius.

Easterton. – The present form of the word would lead us to think that it is pure English, without any change from the original. In 1660 it was Esgartun, which is distinctly from the Welsh Esgair, a long low ridge, and Dun, a hill or fort. How the *d* came to be eclipsed by *t* is not known, unless it was for euphony's sake.

Dykeside is a common name throughout the country, and is purely Teutonic, from the M. E. *Dik,* A. S. *Die,* Dutch *Dijk,* Icelandic *Diki,* Greek *Teikos,* Gaelic *Dig,* a dyke or rampart, also a ditch or fosse. *Dhigh* is the Gaelic verb to raise a wall or a rampart.

Cast/ehill is also a common name in Scotland, from O. E. *Castel,* Latin *Castellum,* and a diminutive of *Castrum,* a fortified place. The Welsh form is *Castell.* Irish *Caiseal,* Gaelic *Caisteal.* The form *Cashel* is common in Ireland and twice met with in Scotland – the castle or stronghold on the hill.

Tomshill, anciently *Tomail,* distinctly two Gaelic words, Tom,

a hill, and frequently found as the prefix in place names ; *Ail* is rocky – the rocky hill.

Star. – This word is doubtless from the Scandinavian *Ster,* Icelandic *Setr,* both of which are contracted forms of the Norse *Stadr,* a place or station, and is found as a legacy from the Norsemen wherever they went in the North of Scotland, the Hebrides, and Ireland, as *Tyhstr,* Monkstad, Ulster, Leinster, Munster.

Randy-gairn, anciently *Raith-gairn,* from the Gaelic *Rath,* a circular fort, cognate with the Welsh *Rhath,* a mound or hill. *Gairn* is doubtless from the Gaelic *Gairnain,* a shout, and often an echo – the reverberating rock or hill.

Shogle, in 1670 *Sugail.* – This is evidently from the Gaelic *Sughail,* a marshy place, or land with surface moisture. The generally attributed meaning is *Sabhall,* a barn, but looking at the early form this is incredible.

Glenlatterach, in 1774 Glenlaterach – from the Gaelic *Glean,* Welsh *Glyn* or *Glann,* and Anglo-Saxon *Glen,* a small valley. *Latterach* is from the Gaelic *Leitirach,* the side of a hill or of a country – the glen on the hill side.

Middleton is another word of Teutonic form, Anglo-Saxon *Mid,* Icelandic *Midr,* Latin *Medins,* Greek *Mesos,* the middle, Anglo- Saxon *Ton,* Scandinavian *Tun,* an enclosure, or as now understood, a town or residence. The primary meaning of *Ton* comes from the Gothic *Tains,* Norse *Teinn,* German *Zaun,* a fence formed of twigs, or a place rudely fortified by stakes, and is brought down to us in Scotland in the word Toon.

Green-ward, in 1702 *Greanwart.* – At first sight it would appear that the first part of the word is simply the name of the colour of

growing herbs, but looking at the older form, the signification is entirely different. It is derived from the Gaelic *Grcann,* frowning, and the Teutonic *Wart* or *Warth,* a watch tower or beacon, a guarded place, or a fortification, the frowning or commanding place.

Blainihall, in 1669 *Blar-an-aile,* from the Gaelic *Blar,* a plain, and consequently a battlefield, and *Aile,* wind – the windy plain or field.

Kirkton is from the Norse *Kirche,* Welsh *Cyric,* and Dutch *Kerk.* The Anglo-Saxon *Ton,* an enclosure, forms the latter part – the place of the kirk, in Gaelic, *Clachan.*

Trochail, in 1514 *Trical,* 1570 *Tricels.* – In ancient times among people who followed the double occupation of tillage and pasturage, before the days of imperial measures, when every community to a certain extent had its own idea of bulk, length, and area, and when the country became more densely peopled, consequent sub-division of land took place, with fixed boundaries. In land as in other matters standards of measurement were adopted. Whether the standard Trichel was common universally or confined to certain districts it is impossible to say. In the North, however, the land was divided into Trichels, or thirty divisions to each family. What the extent of a Trichel was the writer has not been able to find out. Of course this mode of distributing the land is long ago obsolete, but in several places throughout the country whose names begin with the prefix *Tri* or *Tre* or *Tra* or *Tro* we find indications that this system was in force. In Ireland the equivalent was *Tricha* or *Trichas. Trochail* therefore means thirty measures of land, and is evidence of the early occupation of the parish of Birnie.

Grangemouth is not found in old documents. It must therefore be taken as a modern name, from the French and Scotch *Grange,* a farm or storehouse for grain, and is cognate with the Gaelic *Grainnseach,* and the low Latin *Grangia.* In Ireland we find it as *Granagh* and *Granaghan,* all of which signify places producing grain.

Bardenside, anciently *Barrdin.* – The suffix side was superimposed about the end of last century. The word is derived from the two Gaelic words *Barr,* the top, the uppermost part of anything, and *Din* is a contraction of the word *Dinnein,* a small heap, but commonly applied to small hills – the farm on the hill side or on the top of small hills.

Rasherook. – This word comes from the Gaelic *Riasg,* a fen or marsh, and is cognate with the M. E. *Rusche, Rische, Resche,* Dutch *Rusch,* a small, soft reed, usually of coarse grass growing out of marshy places ; and Crook, a hook in the land or bend, from the Dutch *Kroke* or *Kreuk,* Icelandic *Kroke* Swedish *Krok* – the marshy corner.

Wallbrae, auciently *Waldbrae* – from the Middle English *Wold* or *Wald,* German *Wald,* Icelandic *Vollr,* used in various senses as Down, a plain, open country, a wood or forest, waste ground, a field. Brae signifies a hill or acclivity. Probably here meaning the farm on the Brae.

Mossend from the German *Moos,* Scandinavian *Mas,* Icelandic *Most,* Swedish *Mossa,* and Russian *Mokk* – a moss, moorland, or swamp – the end of the moorland or swamp.

Durie, in Elgin and Fife. The *Durie* in Fife is said to have been named by Ptolemy in his circumnavigation round Britain. The Romans only Latinised the names they found. Hence this form of the Welsh *Dwr* or *Dwfr,* Gaelic *Dobhr* or *Dobhair,* water, and the same root appears in *Duro, Dour, Dore, Duir, Thur, A dour,* Derwent, and in Ireland it is met with as Doory and Deny.

Hanging folds, anciently *Hanganfeld,* which is clearly a Norse 9 word, from the Scandinavian *Hang, Hangen,* and Anglo-Saxon *Hongian,* a declivity, cognate with Icelandic *Hengja,* and allied to the Latin *Cunctari,* and the Sanskrit *Cank.* Field is also from the Norse Veld or Velt, a hill. The traditional signification of the latter word is folds, pens for sheep or cattle, derived from the Icelandic *Fjol, Fjalar,* and Anglo-Saxon *Falad* or *Fahid,* enclosure on the declivity. The former meaning is preferable.

Lochbnie, in Elgin and Mull. The latter part of this word is frequently found as a qualifying word to lakes and hills throughout the country as well as to trees and flowers. It comes from the Gaelic *Buidhc,* yellow, and is cognate with the Latin *Bodius,* French *Bai,* English *Bay* – the yellow lake or marsh.

Stankhonse. – *Stank* is an old word in topography, and derived from the old French *Estang,* a pond or linn, Spanish *Estanque,* Sanskrit *Stak,* and is applied to a linn in a river or a pond – Stankhouse therefore signifies the house on the margin of the pond or linn.

Level, – This is an Anglicised Gaelic word from the substantive *Laibh* – the adjective is *Laibhail,* pronounced laval, signifying clay or clayey ground, and is often applied to marshy or wet soil. In Gaelic words the aspirate *bh* invariably is eclipsed by *v,* and *mh* becomes eclipsed by *w.*

Claypots. – The first part of this word comes from the Middle English *Clau* or *Clee,* Anglo-Saxon *Claeg,* Dutch and German *Klei.* The latter part, *pots,* was formerly *pits,* which evidently is derived from the Gaelic Pitt, a hollow – hollows made by digging out clay, or sometimes by landslips.

Wardend, in Elgin and Banff – from the Teutonic *Ward, Wart,* and *Warth,* a watching place. The prefix is very commonthroughout the country. Wardie, Edinburgh; Wardlawhill, Lanark ; Warthill, Aberdeen, are examples.

Foths is not a common name in topography. It is from the Gaelic or Pictish *Foth,* a lake or marsh, and frequently a sterile place. Then we have the adjective *Fothannach,* a place overgrown with thistles and weeds.

Gedloch. – The prefix here is from the Scandinavian *Gat,* an opening or passage – in this case between two hills. In 1667 it *Gadloch. Gat* is found as a prefix and also as a root word in many if not all of the Aryan family of languages. The Sanskrit Ghat, as in the Eastern and Western Ghats in India; Calcutta, anciently Kalicutti – the gate of the temple of the goddess of *Kali;* and Calicut on the Malabar coast present the word in various forms. In the Anglo-Saxon it is *Gaeat,* Gaelic *Geata,* and English *Gate,* all signifying an opening or passage. The affix Loch is a super-imposed addition suggesting the idea of water – thus making the word to mean a water passage.

Coinloch. – The traditional meaning of this word is the loch of the dogs, from the Gaelic Cu, a dog, plural form Coin. This, however, is only a euphonical guess. It is derived from the Celtic *Cong,* the point or end of a hill between two valleys or a tongue of land forming a narrow passage.

Boggs. – Bog is a purely Celtic word, although now an acknowledged word in the English language. We find it used in its proper sense in the works of Shakespeare,

Milton, and Bunyan. As it stands, in Gaelic it signifies soft, but is applied to peaty and mossy ground and a quagmire.

Corries. – From the Gaelic *Coire,* a glen, ravine, or deep gully. It is also applied to a cauldron or a whirlpool, as *Corryvrechan* on the west of Argyll, given by Adamnan as Vortex or *CharybdisBrecain,* the whirlpool of St. Brecan, grandson of the famous Niall, and Sir Walter Scott, in the " Lord of the Isles," says –

"And Scarba's isle, whose tortured shore
Still rings to Corryvrecken's roar."

The proper Corrivrecken or whirlpool is not that between Scarba and Jura on the West of Scotland, but that between the historical island of Rathlin and the coast of Antrim, where the Irish merchant with his fifty curachs or boats with their crews were all swallowed up in this awful cauldron of Charybdis Brecani. The old name has long been given up, and the equally expressive name of *Slog-na-mara,* the throat of the sea, is applied to it.

Paddockhill is not an old word, meaning a small enclosure. It is a corruption of the Middle English *Parrock* or *Parroche.* It is not the same word at all as paddock, a toad, from the M. E. *Paddok,* Icelandic *Padda,* Swedish *Padda,* Danish *Padde,* Dutch *Padd,* a jerker or jumper; Sanskrit *Spand,* to vibrate – whence *Sparca- Spanda,* a frog.

Cockmoor. – The first part of this word is from the Middle English *Cok,* Anglo-Saxon *Cocc,* so named from the bird's cry – " *Cryde* anon *cok ! cok !* " Nun's Priest's Tale, 456. In Greek we have *Kokku,* the cry of the cuckoo; and Moor, a heath, from the Dutch Moer, a moor – the moor of the game blackcock.

Duffushillock, in 1667 *Dobhashillock.* – The first part is from the Gaelic *Doibheas,* literally a voice, but invariably applied to a reverberating hill or rock. We have *Cnoc-an-doibhcas* in the west of Inverness, and *Creag-an-doibheas* in the west of Argyll. As in all ancient languages, so in Gaelic, the adjective usually follows the noun – the echo hill.

Glenlossie is rather a misleading name so far as the applicationof the name concerns the actual situation. For the hollow called the glen is east of the course of the Lossie considerably. The derivation of Lossie will be given under Lossiemouth in the parish of Drainie.

Cloddach, or anciently Clodach, is a word in general use along the coast of the country, and signifies a flat, stony shore, here applied to the shore of the river Lossie, and as distinguished from *Traigh,* a sandy beach. In Gaelic-speaking districts *Traigh* is definitely employed to distinguish that part between high and low water marks, and *Cladach* to that part between high water mark and the edge of the grass.

6

SECTION 6

V.

PARISH OF BOHARM.

THIS parish was at one time partly in Banffshire and partly in Elginshire, but a few years ago, by order of the Boundary Commission, the whole was put under the jurisdiction of Banff. The area is 16,741 acres; valuation, $7,496 4s. Ud.; and population about 1166. It is bounded on the west by the river Spey, on the south by the Fiddich, on the north by Bellie, and on the East by Keith. Benaigen, 1500 feet high, occupies much of the area, and a valley overhung by that hill occupies most of the arable land. The average height above sea level of the whole parish is 450 feet. Being an inland parish and some distance from the sea, the land names are mostly derived from the Celtic element, and are almost entirely free from Norse, while, on the other hand, a few present a Brythonic appearance, suggesting the presence of the Welsh element, but it is somewhat uncertain at what period it was introduced.

Boharm in its present form assumes a Teutonic appearance, but, when the history of the name is made known, it will be found to have sprung from the Celtic. In the year 1000 it was *Bncharin,* in 1200, according to Shaw, it was *Bochairn,* in 1220 it was *Bncharin,* and shortly after it was *Buharme* Somewhere about 1774 it assumed its present form. Shaw makes the word to mean the bend or arch about the cairn, from the Gaelic *Bogha,* a bow orbend, and others have, by adopting his meaning, fallen into the same error. In the year 1200 already mentioned a chapel was built by the Bishop of Moray, called the Chapel of *Bocairn,* which was situated about fifty yards north of the castle, and which, like the tower of Blervie, was built on the site of one of the ancient sheilings used for herding cattle. This sheiling was called a cairn for herding cows, or Bo-cairn – *Bo* being the Gaelic for cow, and is allied to the Latin *Bos,* a cow.

Arndily. – The prefix here comes from the Teutonic *Arn, Ern, Arne;* Latin *Ara,* Basque *Area,* French *Aire,* Celtic *Arcs,* a place, farm, or dwelling, and is found as a suffix in such words as Whitern, Candida Casa, or Whitehouse, Aros in Mull, and Arasaig in Argyll. The suffix is from the Gaelic *Dile,* a flood. Arndile – the residence beside the flood; in this case beside the Spey.

Cobblepot. – Cobble here is not the name of a small boat, but is a corruption of the Teutonic word *Kabbelen,* a bend in the bank of a river, made either by the beating of the waters of the river, or by the waters of a tributary. The word is frequently met with as *Kobble.*

Tomhead is from the Gaelic Tom, a round hillock or knoll, or an eminence.

Bogmuck. – The initial part of this word is often found in land names throughout the country. It is taken from the Gaelic *Bog,* a marsh or fen. The latter half is from the Gaelic *Muc,* a pig, with which is cognate the Welsh Moch, Cornish *Moh* – the pigs' marsh.

Killiemore. – The word Coille plays an equally important part in place names, and is variously found as *Killie, Kelly, Cil,* and sometimes *Coll,* a wood. *Mor* is the Gaelic word for big – the large wood.

Ferrenderron. – This word is taken from the Gaelic *Fcarann,*land, ground, or country. In its topographical use it is applied to a particular portion of land, but is widely used as a prefix. The latter part comes from the Gaelic *Dar, Dero, Deryn,* oak, with which is allied the Latin *Drus,* Sanskrit *Dm* – the oak forest.

Tominachty. – For the initial part see Tomhead. – *In* is the article *An, of,* and the Gaelic *Faiche,* a field or a piece of land – the field eminence.

Maggieknockater, anciently *Magh-cnoc-an-oitir,* from the Gaelic *Magh,* a plain; *Oioe,* a hill; and *Oitir,* a ridge. The combination is most descriptive of the place – the plain of the hilly land.

Tanzie. – In topography the Welsh word *Tan,* Gaelic *Teinne,* fire, is found in the various forms of *Tin, Tinny, Tane,* and *Dinnny,* indicating spots where fires of importance used to be made. They might be beacon fires, or the Beltane fires kindled by the ancient Celts on May Day, connected with the religious observances of the Druids. The affix *Zi* is the Old French for habitation, and was introduced into this country by Catholic missionaries, as found in Sussi, the habitation on high, and Issy, the dwelling on the low ground. Tanzie signifies the place of fire.

Balnacoul. – Baile, a town or dwelling, plays an important part as a prefix in the topography of all Celtic countries, and is allied to the Greek Polis. Joined with the article An it is found as *Ballin* and *Baile-an.* Coul signifies a corner or the back of a hill, from the Gaelic *Cul,* and is variously found as Coul, Coull, Cults, and Cool – the corner residence.

Tomnabreck. – For the first part see Tomhead. Brack is the modern form of *Broc,* a badger – the badger hill.

Knockandu is the Gaelic *Cnocan,* a little hill, and *Dnbh,* black – the little black hill. t *Gauldu'ell.* – Wherever the Danes or Norwegians were met withby the Gaelic-speaking people of this country they were called Galls, or strangers. The Norwegians were distinguished as *Fingalls,* white strangers; the Danes as *Dugalls,* the black strangers. Gauldwell is the strangers' well.

Rottenmoss comes from the Gaelic *Rotan,* belching or shaking, as a quagmire – the shaking moss.

Balnellan is from the Gaelic *Baile,* a town or residence, and *Ailean,* a green meadow – the farm of the green pastureland.

Shians. – The belief in the supernatural beings called the fairies was at one time general among Celtic people. They believed these beings dwelt in habitations in the interior of pleasant eminences, which got the name of *Sith* or *Sithcans* – pronounced *Sians – Shians* signifies the abodes of the fairies or fairy hills.

Auchmadies, from the Gaelic *Achadh,* a field or plain. – There are two words in use in Gaelic for a dog – C' and *Madadh* – but the latter form is more commonly found in place names. *Madadh* is also applied to any wild animal of the dog species. Consequently Auchmadies may signify the field of the dogs or the field of the foxes.

Starhcad is from the Scandinavian *Ster,* Icelandic *Setr,* both contracted forms of *Stadr,* a station or place – the head of the station.

Tombain is from the two Gaelic words *Tom,* a hillock, and *Ban,* white – the white hillock.

Belnagarrov). – From the Gaelic *Baile,* a town or residence, and *Garan,* a thicket – the dwelling in the wood.

Cruach. – This word was originally used to designate a stack of corn or hay, but the application was extended to hills presenting a round or stacked appearance. The Welsh is *Crng,* and in Cornwall it is *Cruc* – the stack-like hill.

Aldernie. – The Gaelic *Allt,* a mountain stream, is usually Anglicised *Ald* or *Auld,* and the alderwood is called *Fhearna,* in which the/// is eclipsed by the combination of the two words – the alderwood burn.

Marchside. – This is a comparatively modern name, from the Anglo-Saxon *Mark,* a boundary, French *Marche* – the boundary side.

Coldhome. – So named from the exposed situation of the place and the uncongenial nature of the soil. This word is very common in the north-eastern counties of Scotland where the soil is marshy or mossy.

Windyhillock signifies a hillock exposed to all winds, especially to the cold north-east winds which blow so keenly down the Moray Firth.

Berry leys. – About 1516 the form of this word was *Bearaglas,* from the Gaelic *Bcarradh,* the top of a hill, and *Glas,* literally grey, but when applied to pasture it is green. The Gaelic for green ground or green field is *Talamh Glas,* and this word would therefore mean the green hill top.

Lochleask. – In 1766 this word was *Lochiasg.* Running water has often got names from the manner in which it flows – straight or crooked, fast or slow, turbulent or smooth. The adjective *Lasg* or *Leask* is from the Gaelic *Leasg,* literally lazy, but here signifying the slow flowing water.

Dowalls. – The first part, *Dow,* of this word is from the Gaelic *Dti, Dnbh,* black, and when found in patronymics signifies a black stranger or a Dane, and by extended use has become to signify any treacherous person, from the manner in which the Danes treated the natives. The latter part of the word, Alls, is from the Gaelic *Ail,* a rock – the black rock or black hill.

Fiddich. – It is locally believed that this word signifies the ravens' stream *(Fithcack,* a raven), and is locally pronounced Fittach. In 1478 the word was *Fidhach,* which puts an entirely different aspect on the signification. This early spelling is from the Gaelic *Fiodh,* wood, which is cognate with the Welsh *Gnid,* German *Witu,* and Anglo-Saxon *Verdu,* English wood. *Ach* is' the Gaelic termination of adjectives formed from substantives. Hence *Fidhach* or *Fiodhach* signifies woody – the woody stream.

Dinnyorn. – The prefix of this word is Celtic – *Din,* a fortified height, and is cognate with the Gaelic *Dun.* It is also found as *Din, Dan,* and *Den.* The latter part, *Yorn,* was anciently *Ghorn,* from the Teutonic Gora or Goran, a mountain – the hill fortification.

Auchroisk, from the Gaelic, Achadh, afield or plain. The suffix *Roisk* was formerly *Rasg,* which is another form of the substantive *Riasg,* a moor, fen, or marsh, or ley ground, or coarse mountain grass – the plain of the coarse grass or moorish plain.

Clay land is a modern name from the old word *Clabarach,* clayey land, and is cognate with the Middle English *Clai,* Anglo-Saxon *Cley,* Dutch and German *Klei,* also allied to the verbs – Anglo- Saxon *Cleofan,* Dutch *Kloven,* Icelandic *Kljnfa,* Greek *Glaphos,* to stick.

Corrie. – Round hollows were often designated by the Gaelic terms which correspond to the English Vat, Kettle, and Caldron. *Coire* literally means a kettle or boiler, and in land names is applied to deep hollows in mountains or a whirlpool in the sea,

Barns is the modernised form of the word *Bearnas,* from the Gaelic Bearnach, full of gaps in a hill or mountain. Bearnan is a little gap. The word is frequently found as Barns, Barnes, and sometimes as Barons.

Strypeside. – From the Gaelic *Streup,* strife, contention, or plunder, and corresponds with the Anglo-Saxon *Strypan,* Dutch *Stroopen,* to plunder. The signification of *Streup* is also extended to mean a skirmish or insurrection. Most likely the place of the skirmish.

Carlnsk is taken from the Gaelic *Curr,* a corner, an end, a pit, or fountain; and *Liasg,* a hut – the corner hut, pit, or fountain.

Caltanach. – The hazel in olden times was a common wood all over the country, and many places abound with it at the present day. Calltuinn is the Gaelic for hazel; *Ach* forms the adjectival termination in Gaelic. Caltanach signifies abounding in hazel.

Ardoch signifies the plain on the height – from the Gaelic Ard, a height, and Achadh, a plain or field – the plain on the height.

Newtack. – How this word came to assume its present form is difficult to make out Of euphonious similarity to the former word very little remains. In 1700 it was *Nadag* – from the Gaelic *Neadag,* a circular hollow; literally a bird's nest.

Popine. – The portions of land set apart for the use of the priests in former days were quite numerous all over the country. This word is the Scandinavian *Papa,* a priest, and means the priest's land. It is met with in the various forms of *Papa, Pfaffen, Papen, Poppo,* and *Popine,* as here.

Mansfield comes from the Celtic *Miii, men,* and *Maen,* a high rock or the brow of a hill. Field the latter half of the word, is a mutation of the Norse Velt or Veld, a range of hills or mountains. The combination here forms a tautology or a reduplication of words having the same meaning united into one from different eources.

Craigellachie. – Various significations have been given to this name. One says it might be Craigdhealachidh, the dividing orboundary rock. Another that it is Craigelach, the swans' rock; and the writer at one time with equal persistency maintained it to be Craigiolachie, the rock from which the Clan Grant shouted their war cry. In 1759 the form of the word was Craigaileach – from the Gaelic Craig, a rock, and Aileach, windy. At the same time, the word is found in another form – Craigailbheach, from the Gaelic Ailbhe, a rock. The adjective also means flint. The word may therefore mean the flinty rock or the windy rock.

Delfur – from the Gaelic Dail, a plain. *Fnar* is the Gaelic adjective for cold, and is applied to wet, marshy soil – the cold plain.

Auchlunkart – from the Gaelic Achadh, a field or plain; *Lnnd* 'J or *Lunk* is from the Norse, and means a sacred grove – a place where the ancient Druids performed their religious ceremonies. *Art* is a contraction of *Wart,* a guarded place. The word signifies the field of the guarded grove.

Cannabnrn. – *Canna,* the first part, comes from the Latin and Greek *Canna,* a reed. The Gaelic equivalent is *Cuile* – the willow or bulrush burn.

Fidde, anciently *Fidh,* which is a contracted form of the Gaelic *Fiodh,* wood or woody.

Rinnochat, in 1706 *Rinagat,* from the Gaelic *Reidh,* a hillside stretch; *Na* is the genitive preposition *of;* and *Gat* is the Norse for a gap or opening in a hill or mountain – the serrated stretch of land.

Garland, anciently *Garlach,* from the Gaelic *garbhach,* the rugged part of a country or the rough bed of a river. The word *Garbh* is frequently met with in topography.

Dclmore – from the Gaelic Dail, a field or plain, and Mor, big or large. There are several Dalmores in the country, all having the same signification.

Burghnamary. – Burgh is from the Teutonic, Scandinavian Borg, French Bourg, a town or city, but literally an enclosed dwelling – often fortified place – and is a contracted form of the Teutonic *Bergen,* to protect. These fortified places were built on isolated rocks, as in Dumbarton, Stirling, and Edinburgh, for greater security, consequently the word *Berg,* a hill, was synonymously used. *Na* is the genitive of the article. Mary is a comiption of the old Gaelic woiti *Maer,* or as now used *Maor,* a steward or bailiff. The old form of the word was *Borgnamhaer* – the steward's residence.

Knowehead. – Knowe is the Scotch form of the English Knoll – the hillock head.

Drakemyres, anciently *Drachmeer,* evidently from the Norse *Drecht,* a meadow or pasture-land, and *Moer,* waste land – the waste pasture-land.

Mulben, in 1669 *Maolbein,* which is evidently from the Gaelic *Maol,* bare or bald, and when applied in topography signifies destitute of vegetation. *Ben* is from the Gaelic *Beinn,* a mountain or hill – the bare hill.

Shalloch, Gaelic *Seilach,* Latin *Salix,* the willow. In the Isle of Man it is called Shell, Welsh *Helyg,* and is to be frequently found in the place names of the country under a variety of forms.

Sonndmoor. – At first sight this word would appear to be English. In 1711 it was *Sundmuir,* which shows at once that the first part of the word is not of native origin. Both in the Norse and Teutonic languages the word *Sund* signifies a piece of privileged land, and in olden times many pieces of privileged land were set apart for flocks and droves to rest and feed on in their journey from one part of the country to another. Soundmoor means the free moor.

Clachnawarren, anciently *Clachnabarphan,* from the Gaelic *Clach,*

Grantown-on-Spey. a stone, and *Barpannan,* conical heaps of stones put up as memorials of the dead, or of any great event, and the word is met with as Barrows, from the Scandinavian Barrow, a mound of earth; Anglo-Saxon *Bcorh* – the memorial cairn.

Forgie, from the Gaelic *Fothir,* land, and *Gaoth* or *Gaoithe,* wind – the windy land; that land very much exposed to wind.

Lochdhu. – Loch, and the Gaelic *Dubh,* black. Adamnan has Latinised this word as *Lochdiae,* meaning the black loch.

Balnabreich – from the Gaelic *Baile,* a residence, and *Bruaich,* a brae or the face of an incline – the residence on the brae.

Holl – from the Teutonic *Holle,* cave or hollow. It is also found as *Hohle,* allied to the Icelandic *Hoi,* Danish *Htd,* Gothic *Us-hulon,* to hollow out.

Cummingston, anciently *Comanton,* and is after the ancient Abbot *Cnmaine* or *Cummenc,* a follower of St. Columba, who died in 669. He wrote a life of the Saint, much thought of by the Irish, but little known in this country, on account of the superior importance attached to Reeves' translation of the life of the Saint written by Adamnan. Several places throughout the country have been denominated after Cumaine, notably Fort-Augustus the old name of which was Kil-Cumin, in Gaelic to this day *Kil-a- Chuimain.* There is also Kilchoman in Argyllshire.

Cullieshangan. – The first part of the word is from the Gaelic *Coille,* a wood. The pismire or ant is generally found in woods and among the roots of trees. The Gaelic word for these creatures is *Seangan,* which is often found in the names of the places where they abound – the wood of the ants.

Gorlioch. – This is a corruption of the Gaelic word *Garluch,* a mole, which, like the ant, has contributed not a little to the naming of the places where it much abounds.

Backdtalloch comes from the Gaelic *Bachdseileach,* the willow brae or hill. Bachd literally signifies the top of the brae or hill, as seen in the expression Bachd-na-bruaich, the top of the brae.

Clach-na-yell, in 1574 *Clach-na-gcill* – from the Gaelic *Clach,* a stone. *Na* is the genitive *of.* Throughout the country in olden times many of these stones and cairns were erected to point out and commemorate both triumph and defeat in many a sanguinary contest. In this case it is defeat or submission, *Geill* being the Gaelic word for yielding or submitting.

Craiglug – from the Gaelic *Craig,* a rock, and the Teutonic *Lug, Luka, Luz,* Gaelic *Leoig,* a hollow or bend – the rocky hollow; or vice versa – the hollow rock.

Culfoldic – from the Gaelic *Cuil,* a nook or corner, and the Gaelic *Foiltc,* a den or hiding place ; also the lair of a wild beast. The word is meet with as *Fail, Foil, Foild.* Another word is *Brocluinn,* having the same signification.

Bauds is a word frequently found in the topography of the north-east of Scotland, and is generally given where there have been clumps of trees or brushwood, from the Gaelic *Bad,* a clump of trees. The plural is *Bada,* and the diminutive is *Badan,* a little clump of trees, and is generally found as *Bad, Bod, Bawd,* and rarely *Bode.*

Tarn. – In 1710 this word was *Taim,* which would appear to be the Gaelic *Tamh,* rest or quietness, but here signifying abode – the sheltered dwelling.

Clackenwells, anciently *Clochenwells,* from the Gaelic plural Clachan, abounding in stones or pebbles, or rocks. Water issuing out of rocks or stony places.

Spcy. – the Romans named this river Teusiss, which is evidently from the Greek word Teukrion, a plant called germander, vulgarly the spleemvort. The oldest form of the word that can be traced is in 1235, when it was *Sfc,* which is probably the original form. *Spe* is an old Pictish word, from which is derived our Gaelic *Speidh,* rapidity or strength, cognate with which is the Sanskrit *Sphiti,* to increase in strength or force, and allied to which is the Danish *Spocd,* Anglo-Saxon *Spowan,* both signifying rapidity. The *Spean,* a river in the county of Inverness, is from the same source – *Spe,* rapidity, and Amhuinn. *Spedlin,* in Dumfries, a strong, turreted, ancient tower on the Annan river, has a similar signification.

Ben-Aigen. – The first part of this word is from the Gaelic *Beinn* or *Ben,* Welsh *Pen,* a mountain. The latter part is from the Gaelic *Aigeann,* an abyss or deep pool or gorge – the ben of the abyss or of the gorge, the latter not far from Arndilly House. The word is variously met with as *Aigin, Aigen, Aiken.* Aikenhead, in Forfar, and Aikenhead, in Renfrew, come from the same source.

7

SECTION 7

VI.

PARISH OF CROMDALE.

THIS large parish is intersected by the Spey. Prior to 1870 part of it was in Inverness-shire. It is seventeen miles long by ten miles broad. Its real property is about $12,000. The hills of Cromdale are on its southern boundary, and the haughs on low grounds were the scene of a famous battle in 1690. In this parish is situated Castle Grant, the ancient seat of the Earls of Seafield, and also the ruins of Muckcrach and Lochindorb. Gaelic is spoken throughout the most part of it at the present day, and being inland its place names are almost entirely Celtic. Few of the more modern names are from the Teutonic, and still fewer from the Welsh. With these exceptions the original language supplies the rest.

Cromdale. – The first part of this name runs through all the Aryan family of languages. Gaelic *Crom,* Welsh *Crwm,* German *Krumm,* Anglo-Saxon *Crumb,* all signifying crooked. The latter part is from the Gaelic *Dail,* a valley, and is akin to the Icelandic *Dalr,* Danish *Dal,* and German *Thal.* The winding valley following the sweep of the Spey.

Lynemore, is from the Gaelic *Linne,* Welsh *Llynn,* Anglo-Saxon *Hylnna,* a pool or lake. The suffix is from the Gaelic Mor, big – the big pool.

Garthkcen. – The first part of this word comes from theTeutonic *Garth,* allied to the Scandinavian *Gart,* and the Gaelic *Garrad,* Welsh *Garrd,* an enclosed place, and by usage has come to signify a farm. The French words *Garda* and *Warda,* also allied to this word, originally signified a fortified place, but are now used in the same sense as *Garth.* Keen, the latter part of the name is a corruption of the Gaelic *Ceann,* a head – the farm at the head of the valley.

Lochnellan. – In 1690 this was *Loch-an-alen,* evidently from the Gaelic *Loch,* a lake, *an* being the genitive form *of,* and *Ailean,* a green plain or meadow – here signifying the meadow on the margin of the loch.

Uig is a Gaelic word signifying a nook, a retired place, a solitary hollow, a cove or den, cognate with which is the Teutonic *Wich, Wic, Wyk,* the Scandinavian *Wick, Vig,* and the Icelandic *Vic.*

Callendar. – It is evident this is an imported word from the neighbouring county of Perth. Anciently the word was Calentyr and Kalentar, and some make this to signify *Coille-an-tir* – the wood of the land – which is improbable, the meaning seems to be the common form *Coille-an-doir* – the oak wood – from the Gaelic word *Dair,* with which is cognate the Welsh *Dar, Dero, Deryn,* Latin *Dnts,* Sanskrit *Dm,* an oak. The *d* is here eclipsed by *t,* in the old forms according to custom when it succeeds the preposition *an.* The oak wood.

Polereach is from the Gaelic *Poll,* Welsh *Pwl,* and Teutonic *Pool,* a pool or marsh, with which is cognate the Latin *Palns.* The latter part is from the Gaelic *Criadhach* (pronounced *Criach),* clay. Another Gaelic word is *Clabar.* The clay pool.

Balnacrieve. – From the Gaelic Baile, a town or residence, and *Craoibh* (pronounced Grieve), trees or wood. The residence in the wood or by the wood.

Balvation. – From the Gaelic Baile, as above, and the Scandinavian *Vatn,* or *Vand,* a lake. This latter part is met with throughout the country in the various forms of *Vatan, Vattin, Vatton,* and *Watan.* The residence near the lake or marsh. ' *Dalehroy,* anciently *Daleroive.* One person gives this word as

Dalcruaidh, but looking at the old form it is evidently from the Gaelic Dail, a valley, and *Craoibhe* (the plural of Craobh), a tree – the woody valley.

Straan, anciently *Strathan,* evidently from the Gaelic *Strath,* anglicised Strath, a valley. *Straan* is a little valley. The valley of the Ugie in Aberdeenshire was in olden times known as Straan Uigie. The Welsh word for strath is *Ystrad,* and found in the word Yester in Mid-Lothian.

Knocktukhan, in Gaelic *Cnoc-na-tulaichatn.* This is in reality a tautology, from *Cnoc,* a hill, and Tulach, also a hill or mound. The Welsh form of *Cnoc* is *Knivc.*

Knockanbuie. – Knockan is a little hill. The second part, Buie, is from the Gaelic *Buidhe,* yellow, of a gold colour, and is frequently found in Scotch topography. The yellow hillock.

Culdreen. – The first part of this word is from *Cul* or *Cnil,* a corner, or the back of anything. With reference to its application to places, it is used in the same sense as the Latin prefix trans is applied in such terms as trans-Atlantic, trans-Caucasia, and such like, so Cul in relation to a hill is applied to the side remote from the person speaking. *Dreen* is from the Gaelic *Droigheann,* a thorn, with which is cognate the German

Dorn, Dutch *Doom,* Anglo-Saxon *Thyrn,* Welsh *Draenen.* The thorny hillside or thorny corner.

Glentulchan. – From the Gaelic *Glcann,* Welsh *Gfyn* or *Glann,* English *Glen,* a small valley, often named from the river or streamflowing through it, but in this case it is designated from the plural of Tulach, a little hill. The glen of the little hills.

Culdrachbeg and *Culdorachmore.* – See Culdreen for the word *Cul, Dorach,* or *Drach* – in both cases is from the Gaelic *Doireach,* a grove, *Beg* and *Mhor* signifying little and big. Culdrachbeg is the little woody corner; Culdorachmor is the big woody corner. *Delyoru.* – The first part is from the word *Dail,* a plain or field. The affix *Yorn* is not directly a Gaelic word. It is the Teutonic *t Goran,* a hill or mountain. The Gaelic for it is *Dorn,* a hill. The plain at the base of the hill.

Fanmore. – The prefix here is from the Gaelic *Founn,* a portion of land; is also applied to the earth or soil. The suffix is from *Mor, big.* The large portion ofland.

Achvockie. – The prefix here is from the Gaelic *Achadh,* a plain or field, and *Cuic,* the plural form of a young buck or roe deer – the field or plain of the deer.

Tormore. – From the Gaelic *Torr,* Welsh *Twr, &* conical hill, and *JMor,* big – the large hill.

Gar'calt. – Garbh, the Gaelic for rough, is quite a common qualifying word in topography, and frequently found as a designating word in the names of streams and mountains. Ault is the Gaelic for a burn – the rough stream.

Airdbcg. – Aird, the first part of the word, is not to be confounded with the word Ard. The former means a point of land, the latter a height. Beg, the qualifying word, is from the Gaelic *Beag,* little – the little point.

Advic. – Mr. Johnston, of Falkirk, thinks this word is from the Gaelic *Fliada,* long, and *Abh,* a river, which is far from correct. This word has a history. *Ad,* the first part, is a contraction of the Teutonic *Abt,* Latin *Abbatis,* an abbot. It is a well-known law oforthographical interchange that the consonantal letters b, c, d, f, g, p, s, t are each eclipsed by a special letter of its own. The terminal letter t in Abt is eclipsed by d, and the alteration has the effect of silencing the b altogether; hence Abt became Ad. Vie, the suffix of the word, is the Norse, literally for holy, but by usage extended to signify a church or cell. The abbot's church or cell, and the ruins of this very old church or cell are still to be found not very far away from the site of the present church.

Deldow, from the Gaelic Bail, a plain or field, and Dubh, black – the black or dark field.

Aultyorn, from the Gaelic Allt, a burn. Frequently this word is confounded with Alt, Welsh Alit, a height or cliff. *Yorn* is from) the Teutonic *Goran,* Gaelic *Dorn,* a hill. In its latter form it is ' met with as *Dorn* or *Dliorn* (pronounced *Yorn).* The mountain stream.

Duier is a corruption of the Gaelic *Dobhr* or *Dobhair,* found also as Dur, Welsh *Dwfr* or *Dwr,* Breton *Duor. Dobhr* is one of the many Gaelic terms for water, which is evidently directly taken from the Sanskrit *Dabhra,* the sea. For this word Ptolemy in his geography uses *Dur. Dobhar-chu* is the Gaelic for an otter, and *Dobhar-fus* is water cress.

Dalvey, from Dail, a plain or field, and Beith, Welsh *Bedtv,* and *Bedwen,* cognate with the Latin *Betula,* the birch tree Many places have received their names from this wood, and as a terminal syllable it takes various forms, as Bay, Veagh, Beith, and Beath, Beathie, and Beth. The birchwood plain.

Balnallon, from the Gaelic *Baile,* a town or residence, and *Ailean,* a green meadow. There is another word, *AilUann,* signifying beautiful, and found in the different forms of *Aluinn, Alainn,* and contracted as *Aille,* but more probably the former, as thearticle n or na would be unnecessary were the signification the beautiful residence. The proper Gaelic form would be Baile-an- ailean – the meadow residence.

Shennoch, from the Gaelic *Sean,* old, and cognate with the Latin *Sen-ex.* Sanskrit *Sana* is often found in place names of the country chiefly applied to natural features and to use. *Och,* the affix, is from the Gaelic Achadh, a field. The old field or fallow land; land formerly in cultivation but allowed to become fallow.

Camriach. – The first part, *Cam,* is the Gaelic word for crooked or curved. It is more particularly applied to glens and straths, and with reference to the sea coast is found as Cambus. The affix, *Riach,* is from the Gaelic *Riabhach,* greyish or brindled. A word frequently applied to hills torn by water spates. The brindled head.

Ballyblair, from the Gaelic Baile, a town or residence, and *Blair* or *Blar,* a plain originally a battlefield – the residence on the plain.

Dalriach, from the Gaelic *Dail,* a plain or field, and *Riabhach,* greyish or brindled – the rough, grey plain.

Lettoch. – In olden times Davach was a measure of land. The word was first used as designating a measure of capacity, and the piece of land sown by the Davoch of corn was called a Davoch. The Gaelic word for half Davoch is Lethdavoch, shortened into Lettoch.

Culfochmore, from the Gaelic *Cnil* or *Cul,* a nook, corner, or back of, and *Faiche,* a field; *Mor,* big – the corner of the large field.

Knock-na-kist. – *Choc* is the Gaelic for a hill, and *Ciste,* literally a box or chest, but in topography a well-defined hollow – the knock of the hollow.

Dellifnre, from the Gaelic *Dail,* a plain or field. The latter part is from the Gaelic *Fnar,* cold, and usually applied to exposed and marshy soft places.

. V-f

Tomvaich, from the Gaelic Jiw/, a hillock. *Vaich,* the latter part is from *Baoghach,* an old Gaelic word denoting the resort of fairies, generally supposed to inhabit little green eminences called *Baoghans* or *Sitheans.* The fairy hillock.

Knock-na-cardich. – The Gaelic *Cnoc,* a hill, also found as Crock, where the combination *en* is changed into *cr* for purposes of pronunciation. Knock is the Anglicised form in which usually the initial *k* is silent. *Cm iic* is the plural form. *Ccardach* is the Gaelic for smithy. The smithy hill.

Achnahamet, formerly *Achadhnahamet* from Achadh, a field or plain, and Annait, literally a church, but in topography also extended to signify churchland ; that is, land which was in olden times set apart for the purposes of church revenues. When the double *n* was eclipsed by the aspirate ;;/ is not known. The word is frequently found in the place names of the country, as *Annat* in Inverness, Hanat in Argyll, Anait in

Skye, all of which have retained the original *n* in preference to the *m.* The church lands. The English equivalents to these names is teind lands.

Achnagallen, from the Gaelic *Achadh,* a field or plain, and *Gallan,* the well-known plant the butterwort – the field of the butterwort.

Clachcndeagle, from the Gaelic Clach, a stone. In olden times and at the present day it was and is the custom in fine evenings for people, young and old, after the labours of the day, to assemble at particular spots, such as on a knoll, or at a large stone dyke, or under a tree. *Deaguil* is the old Gaelic word for evening or twilight, hence these rendezvous were termed Cnoc-an-deaguil, Clach-an-deaguil, Garradhdeaguil, and Craobh-an-deaguil, so that the word is literally the twilight stone.

Derraid. – Doire is the Gaelic for a grove or hollow or dell, and *Fhada,* long or sinuous – the long or sinuous grove or dell.

Auchtogorum. – How the old form *Oc/ulgorm* came to assume the present form is not known ; from the Gaelic *Uchd,* the brow of a hill or rising ground, and *Gorm,* grassy or green – the green brae- face.

Lagg, from the Gaelic *Lag, Lug,* German *Luckc,* cognate with Latin *Lacns,* Greek *Lakkos,* a hollow or lake. It is not common for this word to affix the double *g* except when the diminutive *an* is affixed, which in this case was probably dropped from the form Laggan, a little hollow. It is also found as *Lig, Leg,* and *Luig,* as in Baileanluig, &c.

Craigbcg, from the Gaelic Craig, Carrig, Carrick, Welsh Craig, a rock, and Beag, little or small – the little rock.

Craigdhu is the black rock, from the Gaelic *Dhu,* black. It is also found as *Dubh* and *Du.*

Anchnarrowmore, from the Gaelic *Achadh,* a field or plain, and *Ara,* slaughter or battle or field of battle; *Mor,* big – the field of the big slaughter.

Kuchanroy, from the Gaelic *Caochan,* a small stream. Roy is usually the Anglicised form of the Gaelic word *Ruadh,* red – the red streamlet.

Balnaclash, from *Baile,* a town or residence, and *Clais,* literally a furrow, but extended to signify a ditch, hollow, or grove – the residence in the hollow.

Lyncmore, from the Welsh *Lfynn,* the form assumed in the word; Gaelic *Linn,* a pool, and *Mor,* big – the big pool. In many cases the application of the word Lynn has been extended to signify a hollow or dark dell.

Auchnafairn. – Achadh, a field or plain. The alder is in Gaelic *Fearna;* in Irish it is *Fearn*; and is very common in the topography of Scotland – the field of the Alderwood.

Ballicwqrd, from the Gaelic *Baile,* a town or residence, and *J3hard,* a poet or bard. In this word the combination *bh* is eclipsed by *v,* the ancient form being *Bailcvard,* and in course the 7' became eclipsed by *w* – a well recognised interchange of consonants in the process of Anglicising words.

Glasclwil, from the Gaelic *Glas,* grey, having the appearance of the bark of the birch tree, not the same meaning as when used in the term *Talamh-glas. Coille* is the Gaelic for wood. There is a place of the same name in the parish of Glenelg on the north side of Lochnevis.

Anabord, from the Gaelic *Atk* or *Abh,* a ford or stream, and the Gaelic *Bothar,* a lane, road, or passage. The change from Bothar to Bord is found in Bordcoille, Bordroy, and

Bordgleinn, also Bordaonich, respectively the passage through the wood, red passage, glen road, and mountain path. The ford to which several roads lead.

Druintguish, from the Gaelic *Druim,* cognate with the Latin *Dorsum,* and literally applied to the back of an animal, and by extension has been applied to ridges or long low hills. *GiutJtas* is the Gaelic for firwood. It is also found as *Giubhas,* the fir wood ridge.

Atcndo'M, from the Gaelic *Aitionn,* gorse or juniper, and *Dim,* black – the black gorse field or place.

Onrock, anciently *Od/iarach* (pronounced Orach). The old form of the word was *Odhar* (sounded Oar), signifying dun colour or pale grey, and is found as *Ore, Oar, Our,* and *Otver,* and frequently applied to grey hills, particularly those covered with withered grass.

Rait, anciently *Rate,* and found as *Raith, Ra, Rah,* and *Ray,* and in Latin it is found as Atrium, and applied to a circular moundor entrenchment thrown up to protect the enclosed residences. In Gaelic we have the three words *Lios, Rath,* and *Dun,* having a similar signification.

Anagach, from the Gaelic *Engach,* a track, a fetter, or snare, and by extension applied to any obstruction, particularly to a marsh or quagmire; in this case probably the marshy place.

Rynaballoch, from the Gaelic *Rcid/ie,* a hill stretch, and *Bcalach,* a road or mountain pass. When this word is found as the affix it is usually changed into *Valoch,* the *b* being eclipsed by *v, as* iu Aldivalloch, in " Roy's Wife," &c. The ridge of the passes.

Dellac!ia$jle, found as Delhapel, Delhaple, and Delchaple; from the Gaelic *Dail,* a dell or plain, and the Gaelic *Caibcal,* a cell or church, applied particularly to the rude places of worship erected by the Columbian monks throughout the country, cognate with the French Chapele, Latin Capella, a shrine. When land or a portion of land is used as a prefix to another word signifying church the combined word usually signifies land set apart in olden times for church purposes.

Tominonrd, from the Gaelic *Tom,* a mound or knoll, and *Ourd.* The latter part is a corruption of Scandinavian *Ord,* Gaelic *Uird,* a mountain of a round form and steep, and generally applied to a point or corner.

Sterendy. – The old form was *Sturandhi,* from the Gaelic *Sturr,* the rugged point of a rock or hill, and *Aindibh,* an accident or calamity – the rock or hill of affliction or calamitous hill.

Tomingarn. – The Gaelic *Tom,* a hill or knoll, and *Garan,* a thicket or underwood. The latter part is also found as *Guircan* – the shrubby hill.

Balnafettack, from the Gaelic *Baile,* a residence, and *Fcadag,* the plover, which gets this Gaelic name from Fead, a whistle, the cryof the bird resembling a whistle. The word generally forms the affix of a place name. Often the initial letter / is eclipsed by *v,* and by the combined aspirants *bh,* as Vidog and Bhidog.

Corshelloch, from *Coire,* literally a caldron, but in topography a round deep hollow, just as the crater of a volcano was derived from the Greek *Krater,* a cup, and *Seileach,* the willow, cognate with the Manx *Shell,* Welsh *Helgy,* and Latin *Salix.* The initial *s* is often eclipsed by *t,* as in *Coille-an-tseileachan* – the willow hollow. *r* $, *Polowick,* from the Gaelic *Poll,* Welsh *Pwl,* Armoric *Poull,* a pool, and Teutonic *Wich, Wic,*

Wyk, Norse *Wick, Vig,* Sclavonic *Was, Wies,* a dwelling, and is supposed by some writers to come from the Anglo-Saxon root *Waes,* German *Wiesc,* a meadow. The primary signification seems to have been a station. The root runs through all the Aryan languages. Sanskrit *Veea,* Greek *Oikos,* Polish *Wies,* Celtic *Qwic.* In this country the word seems to have been first used with reference to stations on bays and creeks of the sea, or at the estuaries of rivers.

Waulkmill. – This is a comparatively modern name. The first part of the name was introduced through the Flemish merchants, but the word itself is of Dutch origin – *Walken,* to press or full cloth, and is cognate with the Icelandic *Valka,* Danish *Valkc,* and Scotch *Waulk* – the mill for pressing or fulling cloth.

Balnabodach, from the Gaelic *Baile,* a town or residence, and *Bodach,* an old man. Also used to define a clown, a surly, churlish, ill-natured fellow, and a ghost or fairy. Probably here the old men's place of abode.

Claggersnick. – The terminations *Nach, Tach,* and *Lack* are found in all Gaelic-speaking counties in combination with prefixes ending in the letter *r,* and when the letter *s* is joined to ;- they take the oblique form of *Nich* or *Nick, Teach,* and *Lech.* Theword dagger in topography is taken from the Gaelic *Claigcach,* a steeple, which in its turn gets its name from Clog, a bell. Hills having a round bell-like shape are usually termed *Cloigcach* or *Cloigernich.*

Cragganmore, from the Gaelic *Craig,* a rock, and *Creagan* is the diminutive form meaning a little rock. *Mor,* the suffix, means big. This name therefore signifies the big rock.

Lethendry. – This word was imported into this parish from the neighbouring county of Perth. In 1280 it was *Lcthendy,* and is evidently from the Teutonic *Laen* or *Lehen,* and latterly *Lethen,* signifying fiefland. The terminal syllable *dy* is also a contraction of the Teutonic *Ende,* signifying a corner – the corner fiefland.

Balehnle, from the Gaelic *Baile,* a residence, and *Coillc,* wood. This word assumes many other forms in topographical names, as Kel, Kil, Kelly, Killy. The plural of Coille is Coillte, and is met with in the form of Kilty, Coillidh. The diminutive form is Coillin and Coillteann, applied to underwood or shrubs.

Knockanhighle, from the Gaelic *Cnoc,* a hill. The terminable part Highle is a corruption of the old Gaelic word *Eochaill,* the yew wood, as found in the Ochil Hills and Ochilty, the yew wood hills and yew wood. This word is therefore the yew wood hill.

Croftindam, from the Gaelic *Croit,* a croft, and *Damh,* an ox, and cognate with the Latin *Dama,* a deer. Max Muller says that the transference of a name from one species of animals or plants to another is a curious phenomenon, and not frequently met with. The Greek *Phcgos* signifies an oak, while the corresponding Latin, Gothic, and English terms *Fagus, Boka,* and *Beech* are applied to the beech tree.

Callinduim, from the Gaelic *Coille,* a wood. The latter part, *Duim,* is from the Gaelic *Dumh,* cognate with the Latin *Tumulus,*a raised head, which is derived from the verb *Tumeo,* I swell. These *Duints* are known in Scotland as sepulchral mounds. The wood of the tumuli.

Balmenach. – This word is generally supposed to signify Middle- ton, from the Gaelic *Meadhon,* the middle. This is not so. The Gaelic for Monk is *Manach,* which evidently is taken from the Latin *Monachus,* Greek *Monachos,* a monk. Again from the Greek *Monos,* alone or solitary. The monks' residence.

Croft-na-mollach, from the Gaelic *Croit,* a croft. The Gaelic for curse is *Mallachd,* and is used in topography to signify sterile pieces of land that will produce little crop notwithstanding what amount of labour is spent on them.

Achroisk, from the Gaelic *Achadh,* a field, and *Riasg,* a fen or marsh, cognate with the German *Risch* and the Anglo-Saxon *Risge.* It is also found as *Ruasg,* and as terminals it assumes various forms, as *Riesk, Reisk, Risk, Rcask, Rusk,* and *Ruise.* It is applied generally to wet land, as in the phrase *Talamh- rosgach.*

Phaebuie (pronounced *Faebnie),* from the Gaelic *Frith* (pronounced *Fed),* used to designate a bog or boggy stream flowing through marsh where rushes grow. The latter part is from *Buidhe,* yellow, cognate with the Latin *Badius,* French *Bai.* The yellow marsh.

Auchosnich, from the Gaelic *Ac/iadh,* a field, and *Cosnach* (also written *Cosnaiche),* a labourer or workman – the labourer's field or portion of land.

Dreggie, anciently *Dreggn,* evidently from the Gaelic *Draig- hionn,* the thorn, and variously found as *Droigen, Draen, Drain* and *Dreen,* and as a suffix it is found as *Draighe,* as in Coldraigh.

Gortons, from the Gaelic *Goirtean,* a piece of ploughed land. Itis found as *Cart,* and cognate with the French *Jardin,* Anglo- Saxon *Geard,* and evidently glosses *Hortns.*

Ryecorrach, from the Gaelic *Reidhe,* a stretch of hillside, and *Corrach,* steep or precipitous – the steep declivity or steep hillside.

Glengour, from the Gaelic *Glean,* a glen. The word Glen is the Anglo-Saxon form, and is independent of the Gaelic *Gleann,* which is much older, being in use in this country in pre-Saxon times. *Gobhair* is the Gaelic for goats. It is common to a number of languages. Latin *Caper,* Welsh *Gafer,* Cornish *Gavar,* Anglo- Saxon *Haefer.* This word was at a very remote period applied to a horse in the form of *Gobur* and *Gabur.*

Rynaerach, from the Gaelic *Reidhe,* a hillside stretch, and *Creach,* plunder, spoil. Evidently a place where formerly the freebooters were in the habit of hiding their plunder.

Tiribeg. – In the initial letter of this word *T* has taken the place of *D.* From the Gaelic *Direadh,* an ascent, and *Beag,* little – the little ascent; and in contradistinction to *Direadhmore,* the big or long ascent. The word as a prefix is frequently found throughout the country.

Corriechorach, from the Gaelic *Coire,* a deep hollow or ravine, and *Corrach,* steep or precipitous – the precipitous ravine.

Glentarrach, from the Gaelic *Gleann,* a glen, and *Tarbhach,* fertile, also *Torach* – the fertile Glen.

Kyleantra, from the Gaelic *Collle,* a wood, and *Srath,* a strath. In the word *Srath* it is usual to insert a *t* between the *s* and the *r,* and the word becomes Strath. The same with the word *Sraid, a.* street, which becomes *Straid. Sron,* a nose, becomes *Stron,* and *Sruth* becomes *Stntth.*

Dulaig. – This is a provincial word from the Gaelic *Dula,* a hollow, and signifies a little hollow.

Inverallan, from the Gaelic *Inver,* a confluence of two streams or the estuary of a river. Evidently the latter part of this word is from the Gaelic *Ailean,* a green plain or meadow. The Allan in Stirling and Allen in Ross are from the same source. The confluence plain or meadow.

Gaich, from the Gaelic *Gag* or *Gachd,* a cleft. It is also found as *Gabhaig* and *Gobhag.*

Rynchra, from the Gaelic *Reidhe,* a hillside stretch, and *Crodh,* cattle – the cattle hill pasture.

Cramiich. – The common Gaelic word for a tree is *Crann,* Welsh *Pren,* Armoric *Prenn.* The genitive form is *Crainn.* The word Crannich signifies abounding in trees.

Fioularig, from the Gaelic *Fionn,* white. Common to all Celtic languages, and evidently glosses Albus. It is also found as *Foun l* a." A and *Fin* or *Finn.* The terminal *Larig* is from *Learg,* the side slope of a hill – the white hillside.

Rynedean, formerly *Ri-n-cdean,* from the Gaelic *Reidhe,* a hillside stretch, and *Aodann,* the face, literally the forehead. It is also written *Eodan,* and used in topography to signify the brow of a hill. The face of the hillside.

Lochindorb, from the Gaelic Loch, a lake, cognate with the Latin *Lacus,* and *Doirbh* the minnow, Gaelic *Meanbh,* little or email, a small British fish found in fresh water lakes. Lochs are usually designated after the fish found in them, as *Loch-na-neasgainn,* the lake of eels; *Loch-na-murcan,* the loch of the lumpfish. Lochindorb is the loch of the minnow.

Toberluag, on the west bank of the Spey opposite the Church of Cromdale, from the Gaelic *Tobar,* a well or spring of fresh water, and *Luag,* one of the Columban monks.

8

SECTION 8

VII.

DALLAS.

THIS Parish occupies the centre of Elginshire. It lies to the south-east of Forres, and is twelve miles long by nine broad, with an area of nearly 23,000 square acres. Its valuation is about $6000, and population 1000. The river Lossie, issuing from a small lake at the south-western extremity, cuts it into nearly two equal parts. Several burns discharge their waters into the river, which acquires at certain seasons considerable volume. Dallas Lodge is a modern residence, and the ruins of Tor Castle is the chief antiquity. In a few of the names of the parish we find the Norse element, supplying evidence that the foreigners penetrated pretty far inland.

Dallas is derived from the two Gaelic words *Dail,* Middle English *Dale,* Icelandic *Dalr,* a valley, and *Eas* or *Ess,* and sometimes *Essie,* literally applied to a waterfall, but by extension now commonly used to designate a river. The strath or valley of the Lossie stretching or extending between the Lossie and Lochty on the south side of the hill of Melundy must have been at one time under water. The nature of the soil is peaty, evidencing the fact Among the early inhabitants of the country streams and rivers were objects of special observation, and each has a legend of its own which has impressed its name on the places through which it flows. The legend of this strath being in former ages under wateris that which has determined the name Dallas or Dollas, as it was formerly called.

Aultguhorn. – This word is common throughout the country under various forms – *Aultvern, Aultquhorn,* from the Gaelic *Allt,* a burn, and the Teutonic *Goran* or *Corn,* a mountain or hill. This suffix is found in recent writings as *Tarn,* Icelandic *Tjorn,* Swedish *Tjarn,* which has come to signify a mountain lake.

Loan is from the Gaelic *Lon,* a marsh. We find the root of this word in the word *Lena,* a river of Siberia, signifying the sluggish or marshy river. The English word Lawn is also derived from it. *Lonaeh* means abounding in marshes.

Torchastle was once a strong fortalice, and forms the chief antiquity of the parish. It is derived from the Gaelic *Tor,* Latin *Turris,* German *Thurm,* and Greek *Pyrgos,,* a mound, a conical hill, and Anglo-Saxon *Castel,* Latin *Castellum,* a fortified place. There is another such place on the estate of Balmaduthy in the Black Isle.

Rhininver. – The first part comes from the Gaelic *Reidhe,* a hillside stretch or a mountain flat or a moory level piece of land among hills, and found as *Rea, Re,* and *Rey.* The latter part is from *Inbhir,* which is the original form of the word still retained in Ireland, but in Scotland the form *Infer* has been adopted, where the letter *v* has eclipsed the combination *bh,* and signifies a river mouth or the confluence of two streams. It is seldom used as a suffix. Lochinver and this word are the only two examples which occurred to the writer. The *Bhir* or *Ver* is evidently cognate with the Latin *Ferre,* and Greek *Pherein.* The hillside stretch or mountain flat at the confluence.

Corries. – The word *Coire,* a deep round hollow, very common in mountainous districts. It is also applied to a ravine or a deepgulch. *Coire* is also the Gaelic for the household utensil kettle, and it is from this that it was applied in topography, just as the crater of a volcano was taken from the Greek *Krater,* a cup. Probably the plural form here signifies a number of hollows.

Tomcork, from the Gaelic *Tom,* a hill or round knoll, and the Gaelic *Core,* Irish *Coirce,* Welsh *Ceirch,* and Armoric *Kerch,* oats. The cereal has been cultivated in this country from very early ages, and on account of the fact that, with the exception of barley, it is the grain that requires the shortest summer and least sunshine to bring it to maturity, along with another equally important fact, namely, that it feeds upon coarse decayed vegetable matter, which accounts for its being the first crop grown in reclaimed land, being thus adapted to soil and climate, are the reasons for its early cultivation.

Bellachraggon. – The transformation through which many place names have gone in the Anglicising process, is very evident in this word. The old form of the word was *Bail-a-crcggan,* from the Gaelic *Baile,* a residence, and *Craggan,* the diminutive form of Craig, a rock – the residence at the little rock.

Aultiunish. – So recent as the year 1860 the form of this word was *Aultayuish.* The former would mean the burn of the Insh, from the Gaelic *Ault,&* burn, and *in is,* Welsh *Ynys, AnnOriaEnes,* and Latin *Insula,* an island, which is applied to a holm or low flat meadow along a river, and is found in the various forms of *Inis, Jiiish,* and *Inch.* The latter form is preferable, being the oldest and the most probable. *Ynish,* the latter part, is from the Gaelic *Giuthas,* the fir. This tree has given names to many places in the north and west of Scotland, showing that in former times it was very abundant.

Scottackleys, from the Gaelic *Sgotan* or *Sgotaig,* a small farm, also by extension, signifying a small flock, and the Middle English *Ley,* a meadow, with which is cognate the German *Loh,* Belgian *Loo,* as found in Waterloo. The small meadow farm.

Edinvail. – The word *Eudan,* or more commonly *Aodunn,* literally a forehead, but topographically used to signify a hill brow, is very common throughout the country in the forms *Edin* and *Eden,* and generally applied as a prefix. The latter part is from *Baile,* the genitive form of which is *Bhaile,* a residence. The initial combination *bh* is usually eclipsed by *v,* hence the form Vail – the house on the brow of the hill.

Ardoch, from the Gaelic *Ard,* a height, used sometimes as a noun, and as in this case as an adjective, and cognate with the Latin *Arduns.* The latter part is a common contraction of the word *Achadh,* a field. The field on the height, and so is Ardoch in Perthshire.

Anargate. – In comparatively recent times markets were held in almost every parish. The Gaelic word for an assembly of this sort was *Acnach* in Ireland, *Aenart* in Scotland. It is locally supposed this is the meaning of this word, but as the word *Aenart* has long ago been obsolete, I am disposed to think the word has a different meaning on account of the word Gate affixed, and that it is derived from the Gaelic *Anariadh,* a toll. Thus the word would signify the toll gate.

Goateraigjrom the Gaelic *Craig,.* rock, found frequently as *Carrig* or *Carraig, wA* usually applied to a large rock – the rock of the goats.

Torrwhinnie, from the Gaelic *Torr,* Welsh *Twr,* a round, well- defined hill. *Caithnc,* the arbutus or strawberry tree, is more frequently found as *Quhinn, Cuinn, Queen,* and *Whinn.* It is generally supposed that this tree is not indigenous to this country, but was introduced from the Continent by the monks.

Auchness, from the Gaelic *Achadh,* a field. The old form waa *Achadh-an-cas,* the field on the margin or bank of the river. *Eas* is always used as a substantive, and primarily signified a cascade or waterfall, and is cognate with the Norse *Foss,* but by extension has become to signify a stream.

Snccoth is a corruption of an old term used for a measure of land. *Socach,* an extent of land as much as one pair of oxen or one

A – %

plough could cultivate.

Hatton. – There are several Hattons throughout the country, and in England the word is found as *Heiton* or *Heaton.* In the Pictish Chronicle of 970 it is *A than,* and in 1200 it was *Ay ton.* The initial *a* is subject to aspiration, which accounts for the aspirate *A* being prefixed. The word is found also as *Atten, Aiten,* and *Attan,* from the Gaelic *Aitionn,* the gorse or juniper.

Clashden. – A deep trench, a furrow, or ditch, or fosse is usually designated by the word *Clais.* The word *Den* affixed is only a reduplication or a tautology.

Whiterashes. – This word had at not a remote period been imported into the parish from the county of Aberdeen, from the Middle English *Ruschc,* Dutch *Rusch,* and Latin *Rnscum,* rushes – the field of the white rushes.

Rynagonp. – The first part is from *Reidhc,* a hillside stretch. *Na* is the genitive form *of.* A mouth, beak, or snout is known in Gaelic by the words *Gab* or *Gob,* both forms being frequently found in place names. There is a distinction, however, made,

Gab literally signifying a mouth and *Gob* a beak or snout, the latter being the form used here, and meaning the peaked or pointed hill.

Coleburn. – The prefix here is the old Gaelic word *Coll,* hazel, cognate with the Latin *Corylus,* Welsh *Coll,* modern Gaelic *Calltuinn* – the hazel burn.

Craigroy, from the Gaelic *Craig,* a rock, and *Ruadh,* red, and cognate with the Latin *Ruber.* This termination is extensively used in the formation of Scotch local names. It has an equivalent in the word *Dearg,* also signifying red. The English word *ruddy* is from the root *Rnadh.*

Tapp. – In several parts of the country, particularly in the north and east, the word Tapp is frequently met with in local names, as in Tap-o'-Noth, in Aberdeen, signifying a round mass or knock. From the Norse *Tapp,* German *Zopf,* Icelandic *Toppr,* a tuft.

Soldow, from the Anglo-Saxon *Sealh,* a kind of willow so named from growing near water. Icelandic *Selja,* Swedish *Salg,* Danish *Selje,* and Gaelic *Sail* or *Saileach,* Welsh *Hclgy,* Greek *Elieke.* Found when a prefix in the various forms of *Sal, Sel, Sol,* and *Sul.* The affix *Dow* is from the Gaelic *Dnbh,* black. The black willow hill.

Wangie, from the German *Wang,* Anglo-Saxon *Wang,* a field or strip of land. Found in several places throughout the country as *Wangen.* In the Scotch doric it is *Whang.*

Shade is a corruption of the Anglo-Saxon *Shaw,* Scandinavian *Skeg,* a wood or grove; Icelandic *Skogr,* Sanskrit *Shn.* Also found in the forms of *Scaga, Shide, Scide,* and *Skid.*

Tombrakc, from the Gaelic *Tom,* a conical hill or knoll. The latter part is from the Gaelic *Brcac,* speckled or parti-coloured, and is generally applied to hillsides or upland districts which often present a speckled or spotted appearance. It is also found in the various forms of *Brack, Brit, Briot,* and *Breat,* which in reality is a different word having the same signification.

Rimichie, from the Gaelic *Reidhe,* a hillside stretch or mountain . moorland, and the Gaelic *Maighcach,* Irish *Mait/uach,* a hare, or place abounding in hares.

Bodnamuir. – The prefix *Bod* is common to all the branches of the Celtic languages, and signifies a dwelling. The root is found in the Sanskrit *Abad,* English *Abode,* Gaelic *Abaid,* a dwelling. The latter part is from the Norse *Mor* or *Moer,* Scotch *Mnir,* a piece of waste land or heath.

Buinneach. – *Amhuinneach* is the adjectival form of the Gaelic word *Amhninn,* cognate with *Amnis,* a river, literally signifying abounding in rivers, but is frequently applied to marshy or moist places. The word *Buinneach* has a similar signification, and is from the root *Boinne,* a small quantity of water. A soft, marshy place.

Kcllas. – The first part of this word is from the Norse *Kchle,* a gorge or defile, and is cognate with the Gaelic *Caol,* or as found in some places *Cael.* In the English it is found as *Kelt* and *Kyle.* The substantive *As* is found in *Eas,* a stream. The gorge or defile of the river.

Badymichael. – *Bad* is another form of *Bod* – see *Bodnamuir.* The old form of the word was *Bodmoyseal.* The change took place about the year 1690. The suffix would therefore seem to be derived from *Magh,* a plain, more frequently found as *Moy,* and the Gaelic *losal,* low or a hollow. The residence of the low plain.

Bauds is another form of *Bod.* The introduction of the vowel into the word is attributable to the Scotch language being distinguished by its lengthened sounding of the vowels, as the word is not found so spelled outside the area of the Scotch.

Mains. – The word *Maen,* a place or district, is common to all the branches of the Celtic languages. In Welsh it is *Maenor,* Latin *Mansio,* and French *Maison.*

Brockintore. – The word *Broc,* a badger, is in extensive use in local names throughout all Scotland. The Anglicised form is*Brock.* It is perhaps more often found as a terminal than otherwise. *Brocach* signifies the haunt of the badgers. *Tore,* the latter part, is from *Torr,* Welsh *Twr,* a hill – the badgers' hill.

Bodnapluck. – For the first part of this word see *Bodnamnir.* Pluck is from the Gaelic *Ploc,* a round mass or a flat piece of land, and extensively applied to the topography of the country. The dwelling on the flat piece of land.

Bod-na-Sialker. – See *Bod* as above. Stalker is from the Norse *Stackr,* Gaelic *Stuaic,* a projecting rock or point, and found in the forms of Stack and Stock. The dwelling at the rock or point.

Bogbnie. – The word *Bog,* though a pure Gaelic word, is now an acknowledged English word as well, having found its way into that language at an early date, and signifies soft. The adjective *Bute* i from the Gaelic *Buidhe,* yellow, cognate with the Latin *Badins,* French *Bai,* English *Bay.* The yellow bog or marsh.

Coldhomc. – Middle English *Kald,* Anglo-Saxon *Ccald,* Icelandic *Kaldr,* Latin *Gelidns,* cold. The cold dwelling-place. This name is applied to houses in a windy situation, as well as to those in moist, wet places. It is also applied to places having a northern exposure.

Slackend. – The first part of this word is from the Gaelic *Slochd,* a pit, den, or hollow. The Anglicised forms are *Slack* and *Slock,* where the combination *ch* is hardened into *k* and the terminal *d* dropped. The end of the hollow or den-end.

Slackmaisley. – For the first part see *Slack* as above. The old form of the word was *Slackmaisel.* The Gaelic for beautiful is *Matseal,* and applied to local names frequently. The beautiful hollow.

Branc-hill. – The first part is a foreign word pure and simple; from the Scandinavian *Bronga,* a well, literally a mineral well, andfrequently met with within the Norse range of influence on the northern shores of Scotland. *Brangan* and *Brankanentham* in the parish of Boyndie, Banffshire, are examples.

Rcynavey. – The first part is from the Gaelic *Reidhe,* a hillside stretch. *Beit/ie,* Welsh *Bedw,* birch, is extensively found in Scotch topography. The initial *b* in this and similar words is usually eclipsed by *v* in the Anglicising process. The birchwood hillside.

Tom-na-Moin is from the Gaelic *Tam,* a round hill or knoll, and *Moine,* peat or moss. The mossy or peaty hill.

Lochty or *Black.* – In the ordnance survey map this stream is known as the Black or Lochty. In Adamnan's " Life of St. Columba" the Lochy is found as *Lochdiae,* signifying the black stream, and also *Nigra-Dca.* The termination *ty* of this word is evidently a hardened form of the adjective *Dubh,* black, and probably the old form was *Lochdubh,* the black stream.

Melundy. – The first part *Me* is from the Gaelic *Magh,* a plain or flat. *Lnndy* is from the Scandinavian *Lund,* a grove where the ancient Druids used to observe their religious rites. At one time the belief was prevalent that on the hill of Melundy were the remains of a Druidical circle where they were wont to perform their sacred ceremonies of fire-worship.

Gervaul. – The usual Gaelic term for roughness or coarseness of land is *Garbh,* found in English as *Garrieff, Garry,* and *Gane.* In its adjectival form it frequently forms the component part of river names. The final part of the word is from the Gaelic *Baile, &* residence. The rough place of abode or rough farm.

Silverford. – The Gaelic word for silver is *Airgiod,* and is cognate with Latin *Argentum,* and with the Sanskrit *Regata.* Several places have got their name from this word from the practice of people in ancient times hiding their treasure inparticular spots easily distinguished, and probably this place was so called from this custom. The ford of the hidden treasure.

Tandagart. – The old form of this word was *Tigh-an-i1 Sagairt.* The first part *Tigh* is the dative of *Teac/i,* a house or dwelling. *Sagart,* a priest, is taken directly from the Latin *Sacerdos,* and is quite common in the topography of the country in the form of Taggart, where the initial *s* is eclipsed by *t,* and in the word under review by *d.* The priest's dwelling.

Febbegg, from the Gaelic *Feith,* a ditch, literally a miry place, and *Beag,* small – the small ditch or small marsh.

Conachie. – The old form of this word was *Ceannachie,* from the Gaelic *Ceann,* a head or point or the end of anything, and is' frequently found as *Kin* or *Ken,* and *Ac/iadh,* a field or plain – the end or head of the plain.

Shatebrae. – The first part of this word is a corruption of the Gaelic *Sceach* (pronounced *Ska),* the hawthorn, and *Brae,* a hill declivity – the hawthorn brae.

9

SECTION 9

VIII.

DRAINIE.

THIS Parish extends four miles along the southern shore of the Moray Firth, and inwards for about two miles. It has an area of 6949 acres; population about 4000 ; and valuation $1300. It is bounded on the east by the river Lossie, on the south by the site of the once beautiful Loch of Spynie, on the west by Duffus, and on the north by the firth. Before Loch Spynie was drained, the parish consisted of a peninsula formed by it, the Lossie, and the Moray firth, stretching east and west, and was known as Kinnedar. The two parishes of Kinnedar and Ogston were conjoined about the year 1675, as indicated by the date on the old spire. There are some most interesting caves on the coast, which in former days were the receptacles of many a hogshead of Holland gin and French wine, and the scene of many a conflict between smugglers and the Excise. The site of the ancient strong castle of Kinnedar adjoins the churchyard. The patron saint of the parish was the venerable St. Gerardine, who took up his abode in a natural cave 10 feet square, and adorned with a beautiful Gothic window and door. This cave was in the rock now adjacent to the railway station, but in the course of working the quarries it was destroyed. A spring of medicinal water issued from the rock above the saint's hermitage.

Drainie is a pure native word, which, notwithstanding the frequent incursions of Norsemen, has retained its hold on the place from the first. Its ancient form was *Draigkn,* which is clearly from the Gaelic *Draigliean,* the thorn, not the usual black thorn, but the " hippophai ramnoidos " or seabuck thorn, which thrives so well on the seashore, and of which little or none is to be found in the parish now. The word is found throughout the country as *Draen, Dreen, Drain, Dtynie, Drynoch,* with which is cognate the German *Dorn,* Dutch *Dooru,* Anglo-Saxon *Thyrn,* Welsh *Draenen.*

Janetsficld. – This word has not the signification usually given to it – that of being Janet's field. The old form of the word was Thanetsfield, from the Middle English *Thein,* Anglo-Saxon *Thogen.* Icelandic *Thegn,* a thane, or literally a warrior. The thane's field or portion of land.

Newlands. – This name applies to land recently brought under cultivation. From the Middle English *Ncwe,* Anglo-Saxon *Niewe,* Icelandic *Nyr,* Danish *Ny,* Welsh *Newydd,* and Gaelic *Nuadh,* Greek *Nesos,* Sanskrit *Nava,* new. The word is found frequently as a qualifying word to the names of towns as well as to reclaimed land, as in Newburgh in Fife, a town of considerable antiquity, owing its origin to the Abbey of Lindores in its immediate neighbourhood. It was erected into a burgh of barony by Alexander III. in 1266, and in the charter it was called " Novus burgus, juxta monasterium de Lindores."

Hamlets is from the Middle English *Hoom,* Dutch *Heim,* Icelandic *Heimer,* a village; English *home,* Scotch *hame.* Hamlet is directly formed from the Fresian *Haw,* with the diminutive *Let* affixed, signifying a little village or a dwelling-place.

Paddockhill. – This is not an old word. It was first used by Evelyn, and is a corruption of the Anglo-Saxon *Parrocke* or*Pearroc,* an enclosure, literally a small enclosed park adjoining a mansion, and cognate with the English *Park,* Gaelic *Pairc.* Skeat says the double *d* was introduced in the same way as in the word Poddish for porridge, which is a softened form of pottage.

Over alehouse. – This is a drastic corruption of an applicable word. The first is from the Dutch *Over,* German *Ufer,* Anglo- Saxon *Ofer,* Scandinavian *Eyre,* a border, boundary, or shore, cognate with the Latin *Ora,* and Greek *Horos;* and *Ail,* a rock or hill. The house on the hill or on the high boundary.

Covesea, from the Anglo-Saxon *Cofa,* Icelandic *Kofi,* a chamber or cave, cognate with Latin *Canea* and *Canus,* a cave or hollow; also the form *Canerna.* The sea caves on the estate of Gordonstoun.

Balormie. – One of the Scandinavian pirates or vikings who infested the southern shores of the Moray Firth was *Ormr.* *Baile* is the Gaelic for a residence, hence the word would originally have been *Baile Orntr.* The place or portion or residence of Ormr.

Penrosc, from the Celtic *Pen,* a head or promontory, and *Ros,* also a promontory. This is a tautology, the two words having the same signification, and usually found where different people or people speaking different languages apply words having the same meaning.

Balgreen, from the Gaelic *Baile,* a residence, and the Gaelic *Grian,* the sun. It also signifies a summer-house or bower. It is supposed by some that this word is from *Bal* or *Bel,* the solar divinity and god of light, and originally the god of all power and might, hence in Gaelic forts and fortified places were called *Bal,* from the same circumstances, and thus many places have got their etymon through a secondary channel while the root is still the same.

Gordonstoun is a patronymic word, and has been in the possession of the family for hundreds of years. Robert Gordon of Gordonstoun, who received the title of baronet, was the first in Scotland to get the honour in the year 1625, when this new order was created or instituted by James the Sixth of Scotland and First of England as one of the sources from which he expected to obtain money.

Silverhill. – There is an old legend about this word wherever it occurs to the effect that in any time of danger from invasion or attack the people were in the habit of hiding their treasures in particular places which might be easily distinguished afterwards, particularly hills and streams. Many such places are found in the country, and known in Gaelic as *Cnoc-an-airgiod,* or silver hill.

Siveethillock, anciently *Snithillock,* which is evidently a corruption or rather an old form of *Sonthhillock,* from the Dutch *Znid,* Icelandic *Sudr* also *Sunur,* the south. We find the word in. *Snd-reyjar,* the southern islands; *Znydersea,* the south sea.

Ogston. – The name of the place where the mensal church under the old Chur, ch of Kinnedar was placed. This is not a patronymic word, as might at first sight be supposed. It comes from the Teutonic *Hone* or *Hoog,* a little elevation or corner, allied to the Scottish *Heugh* and the Scandinavian *Haugr.* The dwelling on the elevation or in the corner or neuk.

Greens. – Many of the names of places are taken from the Gaelic word *Grian,* the sun, which in Gaelic is a feminine noun, as opposed to the English masculine, and is usually applied to places where the ancient Druids worshipped the sun, or more recently to sunny spots, which latter are found in Latin writings as Solarium or Terra Solarius.

At-divot. – The first part of this word is *Aird,* a point, in contradistinction to *Ard,* a height. The second part is commonly

Lossiemouth and Branderburgh. supposed to be the Gaelic *Bhata,* a boat, but this is doubtful, as the old form of the word was *Airdivod,* which points to the Scandinavian *Vad,* a ford, and with which is cognate the Latin *Vadum,* Gaelic *Ath,* and the Anglo-Saxon *Wad.* The signification would therefore be the ford point or point at the ford.

Plewland is a modern name from the Middle English *Plough,* Icelandic *Plogh,* a plough. Grimm affirms that he has grave doubts as to whether the word plough is Teutonic. He suspects it is Celtic, from the Gaelic *Ploc,* a block of wood, a stump of a tree, hence a primitive plough. The ploughed land.

Coulardbank, from the Gaelic *Cul,* the back of anything, and found as *Coul, Cuil, Coull, Cults,* and *Culter.* It is often very difficult to tell whether the word signifies *Cuil,* a corner, or *Cul,* a back. This can only be done when the configuration of the place is known. In this case there can be no doubt but *Cul* is the proper word. Ard here means the height, so that the word signifies the back of the high bank.

Stotfield. – This also is a comparatively modern name, from the Scandinavian *Stoat,* an animal, and thus has the same signification as the word *Stag,* which in the English language is a general name for a male animal. It is cognate with the Icelandic *Studr,* Swedish and Danish *Stut,* the ox field.

Kinneddar. – The first part of this word is from the Gaelic *Ceann,* a head, point, or promontary. Welsh *Cyu* or *Cefn,* Greek *Kephale,* and Sanskrit *Kapala.* The second part *Eddar* is from the Gaelic *Edar,* French *Entre,* Latin *Inter,* between. This word enters into a large number of names throughout the country whose signification express position between two physical features. The point between two waters.

Spynie. – The first form of this word was *Spinne.* In 1295 it

was *Spyny,* about 1400 it was *Spine,* shortly thereafter the present form was adopted We find the same root in *Spean,* a river in Inverness-shire ; in 1516 *Spayng,* 1552 *Spane.* The first syllable *Spi,* or *Spe,* or *Spa* is a Pictish word signifying water, but by extension has become to be understood as a running stream, and then rapidity. The same root is also found in the word *Spa,* a watering-place. The name was given from the loch to the east, which should be called Loch Spynie, not the Loch of Spynie, as is generally the case.

Loc/tside is now an inland farm, but when the valley to the north of it was full of water the name was very applicable. This is what those who live on the farm say is the signification, but the more probably correct one is from Dutch *Loof,* German *Lauf,* a stream or current. The farm beside the current.

Sunbank. – This is a recent name given to a farm not so long ago reclaimed, and is so called because it has a fine southern exposure.

Oakenhead. – The old form of this word was *Oic/tenhead,* which ia derived from the old Gaelic word *Oichen* or *Oichel,* water, and it ia found throughout the country in the various forms of *Okel, Oykell,* and *Ochel,* when strictly applied to water, but when applied to places near water as *Ocal,* a large cavern in Ardnamurchan, Argyllshire; *Ochils,* in Perth and Stirling; *Ogle,* in Forfar.

Kaysbriggs, from *Kay,* a man's name, and the Middle English *Brigge,* Anglo-Saxon *Brycg,* Icelandic *Bryggja,* Swedish *Brygga,* literally a pier, then a pavement and a bridge.

Lossie. – In Ptolemy's Geography it is given as *Loxa,* and afterwards it is found as *Laxia,* from the Norse *Laxa,* a salmon. The root is *Lax,* and the final *a,* and in some cases *o,* a river, with a prefix expressive of the character of the stream, is the mostfrequent form of the word in Iceland, Scandinavia, and in the parts of Britain colonised by the Norsemen. There is a place in a turbulent stream in the west of Ross called *Lcamlox,* signifying the salmon leap or *Saltus Salmonis.* It is very common in the local names as Laxay, the salmon stream in Lewis; Laxdale, the valley of the salmon stream, also in Lewis; Laxfirth, the salmon firth, in Shetland; and Laxford, the salmon stream, in Sutherland.

10

SECTION 10

IX.

DUFFUS.

THIS Parish extends along the shore of the Moray Firth west of Drainie. It is about six miles in length and three in breadth, with an area of 9475 acres, and valuation of about $1400. Population, 6000. The surface, with the exception of two small eminences, is level. The old Loch of Spynie when full extended for about a mile into this parish. The old Castle of Duffus stood on the north-west shore of the lake. This castle was surrounded by a deep moat, a parapet wall, with a drawbridge. The rude workmanship of the walls would indicate that the stronghold must be a very ancient one, and is supposed to have formed a place of protection for the Palace of Spynie opposite it on the south-east side of the then lake. One of its earliest possessors, and possibly its founder, was Freskinus de Moravia, whose family became conspicuous in Moray in the reign of David I. Near the place called Kaim stood an obelisk, conjectured to have been that erected near the village of Camus in commemoration of the victory obtained by Malcolm in Moray over the Danes under the great leader Camus. At the picturesque village of Duffus there is a square surrounded by four regularly paved streets, the workmanship, it is said, of Oliver Cromwell's soldiers, who marched hither on account of the loyalty and devotion of the inhabitants to the Stuart dynasty.

Duffus, in 1290 *Duffhus,* 1512 *Duffons.* – The first part, *Duff,* of this word is clearly from the Gaelic *Dubh,* pronounced *Dhu,* signifying black or dark coloured, and is found in a large number of place names throughout the country in the various forms of *Duff, Doo, Dhu, Dh,* and *Dub,* and in such patronymics as Douglas, literally meaning dark grey, and Dugal, meaning dark stranger. It is also very frequently applied to water in which there is an infusion of mud or the dark reflection of the surrounding hills. The second part, *Us,* is from the Gaelic *Uisge,* Welsh *Gwy,* water, and is met with as *Esk, Usk, Oise, Ottse,* and *Use,* which also enter largely into the topography of the country.

Crosshill. – It was usual with the ancient Celts in this country to mark the place where any providential event had happened, or where they founded a church or village, by erecting a cross to commemorate the event – in this case supposed to have been in memory of Malcolm's victory over the Danes. From the Latin *Crux,* Gaelic *Crois,* a cross. The hill of the cross.

Unthank. – It was the custom of the Norse to apportion or measure land by rental, and like the metre in the metric system, the ounce was the base or unit. The old Gaelic for ounce was *Unga,* from which by mutation came the modern *Unnsa,* and is cognate with the Latin *Uneia,* Old French *Uncc,* and allied to the Greek *Ogkos,* a mass or weight, then as now the twelfth part of a pound, whence the prefix *Un.* The second part, *Thank,* is from the Icelandic *Thegn,* a dignitary; German *Degen,* a warrior; Middle English *Thein,* English *Thane. Unt/uink* is thus so much land rented by the thane for an ounce of silver or gold. We find other measurements in such words as *Penningham* in Wigton, *Pennyfeiler* in Skye – a pennyweight's worth of land – from the Icelandic *Pennigr.* The oldest form is *Pending,* having the samebase as the Dutch *Pand,* a pledge, a token, or coin. Then we have *Feorlig* in Skye – a farthing's worth.

Philaxdale. – The first part of this word comes from the Gaelic *Pill,* a small river inlet, and is the oblique or genitive form of the Gaelic word *Poll,* a pool or hole. The second part, *Lax,* is the Norse word for salmon. Philaxdale is the dale of the salmon stream.

Begrow. – The prefix here is from the Scandinavian *Bee* or *Bock,* a brook, and the Gaelic *Strath,* a valley or dale. *Bee* is also found as *Bock* and *Bach,* and by mutation it is met with as *Fach* and *Vach.*

Spindlemoor. – The old form of this word was *Spansalmoor,* which is evidently a corruption of the English *Spancel,* German *Spannen,* to tie, to fetter, from the custom of fettering or tethering cows or horses in a pasture or moorland. The tethering ground.

Gillston. – The first part of this word is from the Scandinavian *Gill* or *Gja,* Hebrew *Gae,* a ravine, and also found as *Goe.* By extension it is applied to a small bay and to land depressions. The latter part is the Anglo-Saxon *Ton,* Scandinavian *Tun,* an enclosure or dwelling-place. Single enclosures became in Celtic times a village, and the village a town, which particularly arose around the *Duns, Raths,* and *Lises.*

Rothills. – The word *Rath* was in Pictish times applied to a circular mound or entrenchment of earth thrown up for shelter and protection, and translated by Latin writers as *Atrium,* and met with as *Rot, Roth, Rath,* and *Raith.* The hill entrenchment.

Waterton. – This word is not at all what it would at first sight appear to be. The old form was *Watnster,* which got corrupted down to its present disguised form. It is from the Scandinavian *Vatn,* a lake, and *Ster,* a place or dwelling. The same word is found almost identically with this in Waternish in Skye.

Cummingston, in 1696 *Cumineston,* both in Elgin and Aberdeen, from *Cnmmeiie,* the abbot who wrote the life of St. Columba, and who died in 669. The word is found in the Gaelic for Fort- Augustus – *Kil-a-chuimen.*

Clashaugh. – The first part of this word is from the Gaelic *Clash,* a trench or fosse, but frequently applied to a narrow dale or hollow ground. The word *Haugh* being superimposed makes it a tautology.

Roseisle. – The first part is from the Gaelic *Ros,* a promontory. It also signifies a wood, and it is often very difficult to determine which of the two meanings should be applied. When such is the case the nature and configuration of the place ought to be carefully considered. In this çase the more likely signification would be the island, headland, or promontory, from the fact that both the parishes of Duffus and Drainie, forming one peninsula, were once nearly surrounded by water.

Shempston. – The prefix here is from the Scandinavian *Heim,* literally a place of shelter, Anglo-Saxon *Haina,* and cognate with the Greek *Heima.* On the Continent and in several places in England this word takes the form of *Eim, Em, Sheim, Shem,* and *Shemp,* and the suffix is from the Scandinavian *Tun,* an enclosure, so that in this as in several other cases the combination forms a tautology.

Starrmoss. – The prefix here is also a Scandinavian word. *Ster,* contracted from *Stadr,* a place or station, and by extension a dwelling. The dwelling beside the moss.

Buthil. – This is purely a Teutonic word – *Buttel,* a dwelling, and found as *Bold, Battle, Bottle,* Scandinavian *Bol*and *Bo,* and is a very common word wherever the Norsemen set foot in the country. *Buittle* in Kirkcudbright. By extension the word is now applied to a farm.

Charleston. – The origin of this word is from the Anglo-Saxon *Charlock,* a species of wild mustard; also found as *Kedlock.* There is a local tradition that the name was given from the familiar name Charles's-Wain, the cluster of seven stars in the constellation Ursa Major or the Great Bear.

Standing Stones. – The latter part is from the Anglo-Saxon *Stan,* a stone. In several places throughout the country an assemblage of upright stones is found. These were usually put up in circles, and were used by the early inhabitants for special purposes

Inchkeil, from the Gaelic *Innish,* Welsh *Ynys,* an island, and now frequently applied to land near water or a plain. The latter part is from the German *Kahl,* Anglo-Saxon *Calo,* bald, bare, devoid of vegetation, and cognate with the Latin *Calvus.* The bare field.

Bruntland, from the German *Brand,* a place cleared by burning, and cognate with the Icelandic *Brenna,* Danish *Braende,* Swedish *Branna,* and perhaps allied to the Latin *Feruere,* to glow. Cleared land.

Sandymoss, – The old name of this was *Skandmoss,* which is evidently from the German *Schwand,* a wood clearing.

Maisonhaugh, from the French *Maqon,* a house. The dwelling in the haugh.

Invemgie. – The prefix here is from the Gaelic *Inver* or *Inbhtr,* a confluence or creek, and is an element in numerous names throughout Scotland. The suffix *Uig* is also common throughout the north and west, and is from the Scandinavian *Vig,*

Icelandic *Wig, Vyg,* Teutonic *Wich, Wic, Wykt* a creek or bay. The primary meaning seems to have been a station for ships or a harbour. This is an imported word from Peterhead, anciently *Inuerugie-Petri* or *Petri Promontorium.*

Pickylaw. – The prefix of this word is from the Anglo-Saxon *Pic* or *Pike,* French *Pic* or *Puy,* a peak. The suffix is from the Anglo-Saxon *Law, Low,* or *Hleaw,* cognate with the Gaelic *Lagh,* a hill. A tautology.

Weddershillock. – The old form of this word was *Widrohillock,* which is clearly from the Scandinavian *Widr,* wood. The woody hillock.

Hopeman. – There are many traditional derivations given of this word according to the fancy of persons who too readily jump at conclusions. It is still vulgarly called *Howdmon* or *Howdman.* Its ancient name was *Hautmon,* from the Norse *Haupt* or *Hoved* or *Hant* or *Hoot,* a head or promontory. The word is found in *Howth* in Ireland, in *Hod* or *Hoddam* in Dumfries, in *Hanna* in Caithness and Roxburgh; then there is *Hounamlaw.* On the Continent it is found as *Hanpt, Hoft,* and *Hatten.* The second part comes from the French *Mont,* literally a mountain, but applied to lofty headlands. The lofty headland.

Keam. – The old form of this word was *Kaims,* latterly *Kaim,* and finally *Keam,* from the Teutonic *Kamen,* a stone. There was an obelisk erected near this place in commemoration of the victory obtained by Malcolm in Moray over the Danes under their famous leader Camus. Or, judging from the oldest form, it may be from the patronymic *Camus.*

Burghead. – The old name of this place was Terryton, and we find it in Ptolemy's Geography as *Ptoroton,* which is evidently his form of the still older form *Tor-an-dun,* the fortified hill or head, Latterly it was supposed to have been a Danish fort or burgh at one time distinguishable on the headland, but is now generally thought to be of Roman origin, as it corresponds with the *Alata Castra* of Ptolemy. Within its limits a Roman bath wasdiscovered, and on the llth of May, 1809, Mr. Anthony Carlisle exhibited to the Society of Antiquaries in London a drawing of a bull taken from a stone found here, obviously of Roman sculpture. An engraving of it is given in the 16th volume of " Archaeologia," page 365. General Roy has preserved a plan and sections of this station. Against this opinion it is observed by Mr. Rhind, in his " Sketches of the Past and Present State of Moray," published in 1839, that it does not appear at all probable that the Romans ever had any permanent footing in Moray. Agricola sailed round the island on a voyage of discovery. It was from this voyage that Ptolemy drew his materials for his rude map of the country. The Ptoroton of Ptolemy appears to correspond with Burghead, at that time nothing more than a headland. The Varar is the river Boauly. Varris may have been Forres, and Teusis the Spey. Not only from these circumstances, but also from the simple and rude construction of the well itself, the probability is that the Picts were the founders of the fort and the artificers of the well. Nor on this account is it the less interesting as a relic of ancient art. We have abundant examples of the Roman art in other situations, and but few specimens indeed of the ingenuity of the Scandinavians. That the Picts held this stronghold of Burghead there can be no- doubt. The very name and the traditions of the battles which they fought in the vicinity indicate this.

11

SECTION 11

X.

DUTHIL.

THIS Parish is purely Highland, and exceedingly interesting and romantic. It is sixteen miles long by thirteen broad, and is situated on the banks of the River Spey. The population is about 1600. Valuation about $6,000. Three miles to the east of Duthil Manse stands the picturesque ruin of the old tower of Huckerath, a seat of the Grants of Rothiemurchus, which was erected in 1598 by Patrick Grant, a son of John, surnamed the "Simple." The Church of Duthil is one of the few Roman Catholic edifices which escaped the relentless destructive energies of the Reformers.

Duthil. – Various derivations have been given of this word. One is *Taobh-thall,* signifying the other side. This is supposed to have been given in contradiction to *Deshar,* where the old church formerly stood, and supposed to signify the south side. This is not so. The word *Deshar* is from the Latin *Desertum,* and used in an ecclesiastical sense to denote churches built in secluded spots, such as the early saints loved to select, and found variously throughout the country as *Desert, Disert, Dysart, Dysert, Dishard, Deshar,* and in *Clachandysert* in lona, and in the old name for Glenorchy. Another derivation given is *Tuathal,* having a northern exposure. These derivations, however plausible, point to only a part or division of the parish, while our forefathers gave comprehensivenames that conveyed a general idea of the place to be named. Very frequently whole districts were designated by the word *Dubh,* black. Hills, islands, and large areas of land were so designated. The word *Dubh* is softened into *Duth, Dith, Di,* and *Doo;* also *Dow.* and *Du.* The latter part of the word is *Alne,* or more frequently *Ail,* a rock, cliff, or hilly land. Duthil is therefore the black hill, from the ridge that runs through the parish. Another derivation given is the " Glen of Heroes," from a legend that the chief of these on one occasion cleft a hill with one stroke of his sword, which cleft is to this day called *Bearn-a-Claidheamh.*

Kinveachte. – This word is pure Gaelic, from *Ceann,* a head or point, and *Beitheach,* abounding in birch, Welsh *Bedwen* and *Bedw,* and variously found as *Beagh, Bei, Vey, Veagh,* and *Veach, Beath.* The initial *b* is usually eclipsed by *v.*

Knockgranish, from the Gaelic *Cnoc,* a hill, and the Teuton'c *Gran* or *Grenze,* a boundary. The old form of this word was *Knockgransie.* The latter part of the word is not common in this country, though found in a few places, but on the Continent it is frequently met with.

Delhoult. – In olden times this word was *Dail-na-Muilt,* from the Gaelic *Dail,* Dutch *Deel,* German *Thel,* and Irish *Dal,* a dell or, as is sometimes the case, a field or district. In the latter part, the *itt* in the old form *Muilt* is eclipsed by *v. Muiltia* the plural form of *Mult* or *Molt,* a wedder. The wedder grazing place.

Lackgluie, from the Gaelic *Lag, Lug,* German *Lucke,* and cognate with the Latin *Lacns,* and Greek *Lakkos,* a hollow or lake, and *Laogh,* plural *Laoigh* (pronounced *Lute),* a calf or calves. The hollow of the calves.

Drumullie, from the Gaelic *Druim,* the literal meaning of which is a back, but in its topographical application a hill or ridge, and iscognate with the Latin *Dorsnm,* and the Gaelic *Ulaidh,* a treasure. One of the conspicuous places where in olden times the natives hid their treasure.

Laggan-tigh-a-gown. – *Laggan* is the Gaelic for a little hollow. *Tigh* is the Gaelic for a house, and is cognate with the Latin *Teetum,* German *Dach,* and Scandinavian *Tag,* a roof. The Welsh is *Ty,* and it is anglicised *Tagh* and *Tigh.* The third syllable is a corruption of the Gaelic *Gobhainn,* a smith. The combination is the hollow in which is the smith's house.

Avielochan. – The first part, *A vie,* is from the Gaelic *Abh,* a river, with which is cognate the Sanskrit *Ab* and the Persian *Aw,* water. *Lochan* is the Gaelic for a little lake or loch.

Aviemore. – For the first part of this word see *Avielochan.* The latter part is the Gaelic *Mor,* Welsh *Mawr,* great or big. The big river.

Carrbridgc, from the Gaelic *Carr,* a rocky shelf or projecting part of a rock; or it may be from the Gaelic *Car,* a bend or curve.

Slack, from the Gaelic *Slug,* literally the throat, but in local place names is applied to a narrow passage or opening between two hills.

Lynardry, from the Gaelic *Linne,* Welsh *Llynn,* and Anglo-Saxon *Hlynna,* a pool, a lake, and sometimes applied to a waterfall; *Ard,* a height, and *Reidhc,* a hillside. The pool or waterfall at the hillside height.

Tullochgfibban, from the Gaelic *Tulach,* a little hill or mound,-51 and sometimes a measure of land; and *Gribban,* an instrument for breaking the surface of land. It is called in Ireland *Grafan,* in which is hidden the Greek verb *Grapho,* to write or engrave. In. the Gaelic word *Seriban* we find the Latin verb *Seribo.*

Lyntarr, from the Gaelic *Linne,* Welsh *Llynn,* a pool or lake,.

and *Tarr,* literally the lower part of the belly, but in topography applied to the base of a hill or the lower part of a valley.

Dalrachnie. – The old form of this word was *Dal-ra-naoi,* which is evidently from the Gaelic *Dail,* a district or part, and *Rath,* a circular mound or entrenchment thrown up as protection round a level space or garden, and is termed in Latin *Atrium.* The third " syllable is clearly from the Gaelic *Naomh,* a saint. The dale of the saint's enclosure.

Shealachan, from the Gaelic *Seileach,* the willow. Literally this is the adjectival form, the substantive being *Sail,* cognate with the Latin *Salix,* Manx *Shell,* Welsh *Hclgy.* Several places throughout the country get their names from the species of wood naturally growing there. The willow field.

Lethendry. – This word has been imported from Perthshire, the old form of which was *Lcthenendy,* which evidently comes from the Gaelic *Leana,* grassy land with a soft, spongy bottom. The plural form is *Leantaidhe.* The form *Leana* is found as a prefix in many places throughout the country.

Beananach is a pure Gaelic word signifying many small peaks or serrated or pointed hills. Abounding in peaks or points.

Delnahatnich, from the Gaelic *Dail,* a plain or level district; *Na,*

the genitive *of* and *Aitneach,* a stranger. The stranger's field or

plain. The aspirate *h* has been prefixed to the last syllable to form the genitive case after the proposition *na.*

Balnacrive, from the Gaelic *Baile,* a town or residence; *Na,* the preposition *of:* and *Craoibh,* trees or wood.

Loggie. – A name very common, both as a patronymic and as a place name, throughout the country. The old form was *Logyn* and *Logan,* from the Gaelic *Lagan,* a hollow. It is also found as *Laggan.*

Bogroy, from the Gaelic *Bog,* a bog or marsh or quagmire; and *Ruadh,* red, cognate with the Latin *Ruber,* English *Red* or *Ruddy,* and is found as *Rna, Row, Rnf, Roogh,* and *Ro.* The red bog.

Slackmnick, from the Gaelic *Slug,* literally the throat, but applied to narrow passages; and *Muc,* a pig; also the heap raised over the mouth of a vessel in measuring, and hence applied to land raised above the surrounding level. Here probably signifying the passage.

Avingornach, from the Gaelic *Amliuinn* or *Abhuinn* or *Avuinn.* The *mh* in the first form is eclipsed by *bh* in the second, and *bh* by *v* in the third, which is how the numerous Avens and Avons throughout the country are arrived at from the proper form *A iithuinn. Gornach* is from the Norse *Gorn,* Sclavonic *Gora,* and cognate with which is the Greek *Oros,* a hill or mountain. The termination *Ac/i* signifies abounding in. The hill stream.

Aultcheanach. – The first part, *Ault,* of this word should be *Alt,* a hill, and *Chettnanach* signifies heads or peaks. The pointed or peaked hill or mountain.

Ellan is from the Gaelic *Ailean,* a green plain.

Mullochard. – The first part is the Gaelic *Mullach,* the top. As a root word this word enters extensively into the formation of place names. *Mullan,* a little top, is the diminutive form of *Mullach.* The latter part, *Ard,* signifies a height, but in this word it is used in the adjective form. The high summit.

Balnafruch, from the Gaelic *Baile,* a town or residence. *Na,* the genitive *of.* The latter part, *Fruch,* is a corruption of the old Gaelic word *Farrach* or *Forroch,* a meeting place. Locally the signification given to the latter part is *Fraoch,* heath or heather.

Lynechurn, from the Gaelic *Linne,* Welsh *Llynn,* a pool or lake, and sometimes a waterfall, as in the Linn of the Dee and CorraLinn on the Clyde. *Chunt* is the oblique form of *Cam,* a cairn, a heap of stones, also a rocky mount, as found in the Cairngorm mountains.

Cornaich. – The old form of this word was *Carnaich,* which is from the Gaelic *Cam,* a cairn or heap of stones, but here signifying a rough, rocky or hillocky ground.

Delfabr, anciently *Dalfahr,* from the Gaelic *Dail,* a plain, and the old Gaelic *Fachair,* shelving land, and is met with only occasionally throughout the country. It is allied to the other word *Faiche,* a field or lawn.

LynfeuL – For the first part of this word see *Lynechurn.* The latter part is from *Fiatt* or *Fell* or *Fjeld,* the Scandinavian for mountain. The mountain linn.

Inchtomach, from the Gaelic *Innish,* Welsh *Ynys* or *Enez,* German *Inscl,* Latin *Insula,* Greek *Nesos,* an island, and in many cases pasture-land near water. It takes the form *Inch* when applied in the latter sense. *Tomach,* the latter part, is from the Gaelic *Tom,* a hill or knoll, and *Ach,* abounding in. The hilly or knolly pasture-land.

Buttangorm, from the Gaelic *Badan,* a small cluster, a tuft, a little grove, or a round hill with trees, and *Gorin,* blue. It is often applied to mountains or hills. It was also used to designate the colours of various natural objects. The green hill or green grove.

Coilnervaul. – The first part of the word is from the Gaelic *Coille,* a wood, and is represented by various modern forms, as *Kil, Kyle,* and sometimes *Cil,* but in the latter case care must be taken to distinguish it from *Cil,* a church. The old form was *Coil-an-Arigeal.* The present form was adopted about 1764. *Arigeal*signifies a habitation or a small church or a cell, and is cognate with the Latin *Oraculum. Coilnervaul* signifies the habitation or church in the wood.

Balintraid, from the Gaelic *Baile,* a town or residence, and *Sraid,* a street, derived from the Latin *Strata.* In topography it is applied to a road, and found as *Straid, Strad,* and *Srad.* The dwelling beside the road.

Auchtalanch. – The old form of this word was *Achatulach,* from *Achadk,* a field or plain, and *Tulach,* a little hill, and found as *Tilly, Tully,* and *Tuloch;* also as *Tealach.* The hill field.

Lochgorm, from the Gaelic *Loch,* a lake, and *Gorm,* blue. The loch of the blue water.

Lochanhully, from the Gaelic *Lochan,* a little lake. The latter part of the word is from the old Gaelic *Uladh,* a tomb or cairn. It is applied to a stone altar from the ancient practice of devotees of makingtheir devotions on tombstones. The loch of the tomb or cairn.

Chruich, from the Gaelic *Cruach,* the primary signification of which is a stack or rick, but in topography it is applied to hills of a round or stacked form.

Gallovie, or sometimes *Gollivie.* – The word *Gall* has been used in Scotland from very remote times to denote a stranger or foreigner. It is frequently applied in another sense – that of a stone pillar or a rocky mountain or hill. Here it is used in the latter sense. The rock or pillar beside the water.

Inchline, from the Gaelic *Innis,* an island or pasture-land near water, and when applied to pasture-land takes the form of *Inch,* and the Gaelic *Linn,* a pool or lake. The pasture-land beside the linn.

Corrinch, from the Gaelic *Coire,* a ravine, hollow, or whirlpool.

There *in* another word much resembling this – *Cora* or *Coradh,* a weir across a river. For the latter part of the word see Inchline.

Ballagan, from the Gaelic *Baile,* a residence, and *Lagan,* a little hollow. The residence in the little hollow.

Delbuiack, from the Gaelic *Dail,* a field or plain, and *Bnidheag,* a yellow flower. The field of the yellow flowers.

Dochlygie. – The first part, *Doch,* of this word is a contraction of the Gaelic *Dabhoch,* a farm; in olden times applied strictly to a farm sufficient to pasture a certain number of cattle. In the Hebrides it is three hundred and fifty. The latter part, *Lygie,* is from the old Gaelic *Liagan,* the diminutive of *Liag,* a standing stone or the side of a mountain or hill. The hillside farm.

N *Balnaconeagh,* from the Gaelic *Baile,* a residence, and *Coin-t neamhe,* a meeting. The meeting house. Such places were so named at cross roads in olden times or where people used to meet to discuss any matter of importance.

Docharn. – For the first part of this word see the word *Dochlygie.* The latter part, *Am,* is from the Teutonic *Arn,* a home, Latin *Ara,* French *Aire,* Gaelic *Arcs.* The home farm.

Kinchurdy, from the Gaelic *Ceann,* a head or point of land, and found as *Kin* or *Ken* ; *Carr,* a rock, and *Dubh,* black. The head or end of the black rock.

Inverlaidnan, from the Gaelic *Inver,* and found as *Inbhir* and *Inner,* a river confluence or a creek at the mouth of a river. The middle part is from the Gaelic *Liath,* literally grey, and applied to the silvery colour of water. When prefixed to the letters or *a* it invariably assumes the form *Laid or Lead or Led,* in place of *Liath.* The latter part, *Nan,* is a contraction of *Amhuinn,* a river. The mouth or confluence of the silvery stream.

Ielv. – This is rather a peculiar word, surrounded as it is with Gaelic names, and points to a later date than the names of the other places in the parish. It is from the Gaelic *Elv* or *Elf,* a river. It is not frequent in the place names of Scotland, but is common on the Continent, and is found in such names as *Alf, Alb, Elbe, Elben. Laagenely,* the river in the hollow; *Dolelf,* the valley river; and *Elbing,* a town on the river.

Forigen, from the Gaelic *Fothir* (pronounced for), land, and *Elgin,* to oppress; *Eigneach,* an oppressor. The oppressor's land. That is to say, land reclaimed by excessive labour, without remuneration therefor.

Garbhahor. – The first part of this word is from the Gaelic *Garbh,* rough, and is frequently found as an attribute to place names. The latter part is from the Gaelic *Saothair,* labour. The old form was *Garbh-haothair,* in which the initial j of the proper root is eclipsed by the aspirate *h,* and by extension was dropped altogether. The rough labour.

Avchttrchtper. – The initial part of this word is from the Gaelic *Uuchdar,* and found as *Auchter, Ochter,* Welsh *Uchder,* the upper part or the summit, and is sometimes anglicised *water.* The second part is from the Gaelic *Ceap,* the top of a hill or a stake or block, and is cognate with the Latin *Cippus,* a sharp stake, and with the Welsh *Cyff,* and is found as *Kip* and *dp.* The last syllable *er* is a contraction of *Tir,* land, and the proper form of the word is *Uachdar-cheap-tir,* the first two syllables forming a tautology. The summit of the land.

Ess is the Gaelic for a waterfall. There are two nominative forms of this word, *Ess* and *Ass*; the genitive is *Essa* and *Essy,* and in these forms it enters largely into the place names of the country.

Rymagag, from the Gaelic *Reidhe,* a hillside stretch, and *Magach,* abounding in fields. The old form was *Reid/unagach,* which literally signifies a stretch or series of fields.

Balnafettach. – For this word see the parish of Abemethy.

Tonmtighleach, from the Gaelic *Tom,* a round hill or knoll, and *Tulach* or *Tulaich,* a hillock; also a tautology.

12

SECTION 12

XI.

DYKE AND MOY.

THESE two Parishes were united in 1618. This united parish is an irregular, four-cornered figure, on the margin of the Moray Firth, to an extent of six miles, and extending southwards nearly the same length. A great portion of it is fertile and highly cultivated. Along the coast is that extensive sandy desert known as the Culbin or Maviston Sandhills. Hector Boethius represents this desert as produced by the same inundation of the the sea which swept away the estate of Earl Goodwin in Kent in 1100, now known as the disastrous Goodwin Sands. Since the original devastation the sea appears to have been encroaching considerably on the coast, and the evil extended by the blowing of the sand inland. These sandhills were originally piled up in three great hills below Maviston, in the parish of Auldearn; and from this great reservoir the sand has been drifted towards the northeast in such enormous quantities that the barony of Culbin, and anciently known as " the granary of Moray," was literally and wholly buried under it about three hundred years ago. The lands were covered to a depth of several feet between the years 1670 and 1695, and the estate so much destroyed, that the proprietor petitioned Parliament to be exempted from paying the ordinary public dues. The removal of the sand to Culbin is said to havebeen facilitated and accelerated by the country people pulling up bent from the ground in the parishes of Dyke and Auldearn, and the practice was, in consequence, prohibited by Act of Parliament. In the churchyard of Dyke is an old tombstone belonging to the family, thus remorsely disinherited. On the upper part of the stone are the initials V K. E. I., and date 1613, after which runs the following legend: –

Valtir Kinnaird, Elizabeth Innes.
" The builders of this bed of stane
Are Laird and Lady of Cowbine,
Quhilk tua and theirs, quhane braithe is gane,
Pleis God, vil sleip this bed vithin."

The heath of Hardmoor, which adjoins the now sterile district of Culbin, is celebrated as the place where Macbeth was met by the Weird Sisters while he journeyed with Banquo from the Western Isles to meet King Duncan at the Castle of Forres.

Dyke. – This place was so called from the fact that it is the site of an ancient camp, and is taken from the Middle English *Dik,* Anglo-Saxon *Die,* Dutch *Dijk,* Icelandic *Diki,* Greek *Teixos,* and Sanskrit *Dehi,* a wall or rampart, a trench and embankment.

Moy. – This word was the ancient name, and is derived from the Gaelic *Magh,* a plain or level track of coujitry. It perhaps is one of the oldest Gaelic words, and Latinised *Magus.* The modern Gaelic is *Ma-chair,* that is *Magh-thir,* the level track of land. It is variously found as *Magh, Moy, Ma,* and *Mag*; also as *Maw,*

Whitemire is a recent name, the old form being *Whitemer,* which evidently signifies the white lake, from the Middle English *Mere,* Dutch *Meer,* Icelandic *Marr,* German *Mcer,* Welsh *Mor,* Gaelic *Muir,* Latin *Mare.* The original sense, according to Skeat, is " dead," once a pool of stagnant water, also the waste ocean.

Bankhead, from the Middle English *Bankc* or *Boncke,* a mound of earth, Dutch *Banck,* Icelandic *Bakki,* the end or head of a bank of earth.

Brodie, in 1311 *Brody,* which is evidently from the Gaelic *Brodha,* a point, a spot, a level piece of land. The same root is found in *Brodiesord,* in Banffshire, which signifies a level piece of land at the base of the Ord hill.

Bineness, from the Gaelic *Beinn,* a mountain or hill, and the Scandinavian *Noes,* Anglo-Saxon *Naes,* French *Ness,* and English *Ness,* a promontory. The high headland.

Kintessack. – The old form of this word was *Kintesk,* from the Gaelic *Ceann,* and frequently found as *Kin, Ken,* and *Cin,* a headland, and *Teasg,* boisterous, wind, storm, or furious waves. The stormy head or cold place.

Dafoey, from the Gaelic *Dail,* Dutch *Deel,* a plain or district. The latter part of the word comes from *Beithc,* the birch. The plain of the birch wood.

Logiebuchnie. – This is evidently in a disguised form the word *Logiebuchan,* from the Gaelic *Lag, Lug,* a hollow, cognate with the Latin *Lacus,* a lake, Greek *Lakkos.* In the Book of Deer, about 1295, the word Buchan is found as *Bomvan,* in 1601 as *Baughan,* but an older form still is *Boc/ion,* and taking this as the most approximately correct one, the word would be derived from the Gaelic *Bochthonu,* a surge or billow, a swelling wave, hence by extended use the undulating land. This part of Aberdeenshire once formed a county of itself, and an earldom which was vested in the chief of the Cummins, until their forfeiture in 1309 The alternately undulating and hollow land.

Broadshaw, from the Middle English *Brood,* Dutch *Breed,* Icelandic *Breidr,* broad, and *Shaw,* a thicket, Icelandic *Skogr,*Swedish *Skog,* Danish *Skov,* Sanskrit *Sku.* The original signification of this root seems to be a covering or shelter. The broad wood or thicket.

Darnaway. – In 1453 it was *Tar/tewa;* 1498 *Darnway,* from the old Gaelic *Dair* or *Doire,* which are, however, more strictly applied to clumps of wood or groves than to the oak species. The Latin *Drus* and Sanskrit *Dru* are cognate with it. The latter part comes from the Gaelic *Baigh,* a noble, hence the phrase *Duine Baighcach,* a nobleman. The nobleman's oak wood or forest. Adjoining the modern mansion is the princely hall built by Earl Randolph, Regent of Scotland during the minority of David Bruce. Here Mary Queen of Scots held the court in 1564. Among the pictures is one of the " Bonny Earl of Moray, who was murdered at Doni- bristle, in the county of Fife, in 1592, on the 7th of February. The Earl of Moray was cruelly murdered by the Earle of Huntly at his house in Dunnibrissell."

" He was a braw gallant,
And he played at the glove ;
And the bonny Earl of Moray.
Oh! he was the Queen's love."

Suable. – The old form of this word was *Chnaip,* which is evidently from the Gaelic *Cnaip,* the plural, and *Cnap,* the singular for a hill of a round form. The aspirates *ch* are eclipsed by *s* in the anglicising process, the former being pronounced hard, like *k* in Gaelic, but soft like *s* in English. *Chnaipal,* or *Ghnaipach,* abounding in round hills.

Craigfield, from the Gaelic *Craig* or *Carrig,* a rock. *Creagach* is the adjective form, and means rocky, and *Field,* from the Middle English *Feld,* Dutch *Veld,* a field. The rocky field.

Bogs, from the Gaelic *Bog,* soft or marshy, hence the Gaelic*Bogan,* a quagmire. Another word for a quagmire is *Snil- chruitheach.*

Crowhall, from the Gaelic *Crodh* (pronounced *Cro),* a dowry. The word also signifies cattle, and there is another word *Cro,* signifying a cattle fold. The bequeathed hall.

Feddau, from the Gaelic *Feadan,* a small stream; also applied to a conduit or to a crevice in a rock

Kineorth, from the Gaelic *Ceann,* a head, and found as *Kin* and *Ken.* The latter part was formerly *Sgarth,* from the Gaelic *Sgarta,* a division. The dividing headland or the dividing hill.

Earnhill. – For *Earn,* the first part of this word, see the parish of Alves. The hill beside the river Findhorn.

Tearie. – The old form was *Tearvie,* which is evidently from the Gaelic *Tir,* land, and the Scandinavian *Vie,* a church. The church lands.

Carse, a term applied in Scotland to low ground on the banks of rivers, and cognate with the Welsh *Cors,* a bog.

Well/till. – This is only a modern form, given from the fact that a well, supposed at one time to possess medicinal properties, issues out of the hill,

Mudhall. – This is an Anglo-Saxon corruption of the old word *Mothill* or *Moothill,* a place of assembly. We find it in Moothill, near Aberdeen, Motehill in Perth, Almoot, which has been corrupted into Old Maud, near Peterhead. The Gaelic for Bute is *Baile-mhoid,* and also extended *Boid-enoc-a-mhoid,* in Lochcarron.

Boathill. – This is from the Teutonic *Buttclor Bottle,* a dwelling. The word is found as *Bold, Battle,* and *Blod.* Battlehill, near Huntly, is from this word. Cognate with it is the Norse *Bol* and *Bo.*

Blinkbonny. – The first part of this word is from the French*Blanc,* German *Blanc,* Anglo-Saxon *Blank,* white, and found in the various forms of *Blenk, Blink,* and *Blnnk.* The latter part is not the English adjective *Bonny,* but is from the Gaelic *Ban,* a hill or height, and found in Wales as *Fan,* where by mutation the *b* becomes/, as in *Cefn-y-fan* and *Tal-y-fan.* The white hill.

Mnirside, from the Scandinavian *Moer* or *Mor,* Scotch *Muir,* waste land or heath. The side of the muir.

Abbotshill, from the Syriac *Abba,* literally a father, Latin *Abbatis,* Teutonic *Abt,* and were introduced into the languages of Europe in connection with the Monastic system and are attached to names of places belonging to church lands. These words are frequently found throughout the country in the various forms of *Abt, Abs, Ab, Abdie, Ad.* The Gaelic *Uag* is the Irish form. The abbot's hill.

Banarach, from the Gaelic *Banaireach,* a sheep fold or an enclosure where sheep are milked, and the milkmaid is termed *Banarach.*

Berry Icy. – The Gaelic pronunciation of this is *Bearradh-liath,* from the Gaelic *Bearradh,* the top of a hill or rock, and the Gaelic *Liath,* grey. The grey hill or rock.

Darklass. – The old form of this word was *Dcarglas,* which comes from the Gaelic *Deargail,* a red place. Our forefathers generally designated places by their most obvious characteristic. Every name denoting the feature that most strongly attracted attention. The red land.

Ellands, from the Anglo-Saxon *Ealand,* Dutch *Eylandt,* literally an island, and is applied to tracts of land in the same sense as Innish.

Broom, formerly *Brem,* which is the Dutch for the plant broom. *Whitenme.* – The prefix here is pure English, but the latterpart, *Unie,* is the much disguised word *Oync* or *Oven,* and found in the various forms of *Ouyn, Ovyn, Owyn, Une, Unie,* as here; *Ean, Een,* all of which signify a soft, marshy place. The white marsh.

Clodiemoss, from the Middle English *Clot, Clotte,* Scandinavian *Clod,* Danish *Klode,* Icelandic *Klot,* German *Kloss,* a ball of earth. The moss abounding in clods.

Flockleys, from the Middle English *Flok,* Icelandic *Floke,* Danish *Flok,* Swedish *Flock,* a herd of sheep or cattle, and the Middle English *Lea, Lay, Ley,* untilled land. The flock pasture-land.

Grangegreen, from the French *Grange,* a farm or storehouse for grain. The Gaelic is *Grainnseach,* and cognate with both the Latin *Granaria* and *Grannm*; and the Middle English *Green,* Dutch *Groen,* Icelandic *Graenn,* the colour of growing herbs, and might be defined the fertile farm.

Bernery, from the Gaelic *Bearna* or *Bearu,* a gap, and usually applied to a gap in a hill or mountain, but also applied to a greater depression than the surrounding land,

and *Airidh* (pronounced *ery),* hill pasture, or a level green among hills; also a summer residence for herdsmen, a shealing. The green hollow.

13

SECTION 13

XIL

EDENKILLIE.

THIS Parish is pastured and hilly, but not mountainous, the highest hill, the Knock of Moray, being of small elevation. It lies on the right bank of the Findhorn, and is watered by the Divie and other streams tributary to the Findhorn. On the banks of the Findhorn and Divie are some of the most romantic rural scenes which wood, water, rock, and variety of ground can produce. The natural woods are very extensive, and the ancient forest of Darnaway covers about 700 acres, and farther up the river is the wood of Dundaff. Southwards up the Dorback is Lochindorb, in the middle of which is an island, with the ruins of Lochindorb Castle, formerly a place of great strength. It was blockaded by Sir Andrew Moray the Regent during David Bruce's captivity in England, and Edward III. in the following year honoured it by raising the siege. It was afterwards used as a State prison. The Uoune Hill of Relugas is a conical hill, round a great part of which runs the Divie in a deep, rocky channel. On the summit are the remains of a strong fortress of antiquity, beyond the period of authentic history. Higher up the Divie stands the Castle of Dunphail upon a rock of singular appearance. It formerly belonged to the Cummings. The singular bridge of Rannoch hereis also of great antiquity, which traditionally derives its name from the illustrious Randolph Earl of Moray and Regent of Scotland.

Edenkillie. – The first part of this word is from the Gaelic *Eudan,* the face, literally a brow; hence by extension it is applied to the face of a hill. It is also found as *Aodann,* and contracted to *Edin, Eden, Edan,* and *Edn.* The latter part is from the Gaelic *Coille,* a wood, and in topography takes the forms of *Kel, Kil, Kelly, Killy,* and *Kyle,* the wood. Signifies the woody hillside or braeface.

Tomdow, from the Gaelic *Tom,* a round hill or knoll, and *Dhu* or *Du,* black. The black hill. This name is very frequently met with in the Gaelic-speaking districts of Scotland, and is quite expressive of this hill.

Tullyglens. – The prefix here is from the Gaelic *Tulach,* a little hill or mound, and variously found as *Tulla, Tullow, Tnlly,* and *Tulli.* In an Irish glossary it is given as the equivalent of *Bri,* which is another word for a little hill, and cognate with which is the English *Brae.* The latter part is from the English *Glen,* and has the same signification as the Gaelic *Gleann,* and though nearly identical in form, the one has not been derived from the other, the one being Anglo-Saxon, and of much later date than the Gaelic *Gleann,* Welsh *Glyn.* The hill glen.

Lougley. – The old form of this word was *Longleith,* which is evidently from the old Pictish word *Luinge,* a place of encampment. From this word has come the modern Gaelic word *Lonn,* a fortress- or stronghold. The latter part is a corruption of the old word *Lios* or *Lis,* now signifying a garden or an enclosure, but literally and formerly strictly applied to a fortification. The entrenched encampment.

Craigroy, from the Gaelic *Craig* or *Carrig,* a rock, and *Rnadh,*red, reddish, and is equivalent to and cognate with the Latin *Ruber.* It is extensively used as a qualifying word. The red rock.

Dunphail, from the Gaelic *Dun,* the primary signification of which is strong or firm. In Latin writings it is often found as the equivalent of *Firmus* and *Fortis,* and in Gaelic it is used as the equivalent of *Lis,* a stronghold. It also glosses *Arx&nA Castntm,* and Adamnan writes it as *Munitio.* It is found in other languages as well as the Celtic. Welsh *Din,* German *Zun.* In recent names it assumes the forms of *Dun, Doon,* and *Don.* The latter part, *Phail,* is an appendix from the Scandinavian *Fiall* or *Fjold,* a mountain or mountain range. The Norsemen, after lauding upon the Scottish coast, would have heard of the strength of this hill fortress, and would have designated the hill by their own word; hence the hill fortress.

Berryley. – For this word see the parish of Dyke and Moy.

Redstean. – Where the Norsemen had settlements this word *Steen,* literally a rock or stone, but in topography sometimes applied to a rock fortress, often marks the site of the grave of one of their heroes. The red rock or stone or fortress.

Dallasbrac/tty. – The first part is from *Dal,* a plain or district. Dutch *Dcel,* German *Theil,* Irish *Dal,* and is also applied to the river which flows through the district. The second part is *Eas* or *Ess,* literally a waterfall, but by extension applied to a rapid stream or river. The third part, *Brachty,* is from the Gaelic *Braich* or *Brach,* malt, literally fermented grain, and often applied to places where illicit stills were erected. Brackla Distillery gets its name from this word.

Conicaiel. – The old form of this word was *Cong-a-Caibhail,* which lets us at once into the signification of the word. The word *Cong* is an old Gaelic word for a habitation. It was a commonword with the old monks in the form of *Congel.* The modern Gaelic is *Cat,* and is found in the next part, *Caibeal,* a chapel. The church habitation or the monks' habitation.

Meiklegreen. – The initial part of this word is from the Scandinavian *Mickla* and *Mycel,* Scotch *Muckle* or *Mickle,* and signifies great. It is frequently met with on the Continent, and particularly applied to fortresses, mountains, and marshes.

Regall is from the Gaelic *Reidh,* a plain or level field, and more commonly employed to signify a mountain flat, and Anglicised *Rea, Re,* and *Ray,* and the second part is from the Gaelic *Ail,* a hill or rock. The smooth hill or rock.

Bogney. – The old form of this word was *Bognach,* which comes from the Gaelic *Bog,* signifying soft or marshy. *Nach,* the latter part, is an adjectival termination formed from substantives, and in the Anglicising process has assumed the new form *Ncy.* Thus *Alulad* is the Gaelic substantive sorrow. *Muladach* is sorrowful, *Gaol,* love, *Gaolach,* lovely. The soft place.

Oichquhorn. – The first part *Oich* is from the obsolete Gaelic word *Oiche,* water, as found in the Oich river, the Oichel, and Loch Oich. It is also found as *Ock, Ocker, Ockc, Eck,* and *Uich.* The latter part of the word is from the Gaelic *Caru,* a mound, and by extension applied to a stack-like hill. The genitive form is *Chuirn*; hence the old form of the word would have been *Oich-a- Chuirn.* The mountain stream or the mountain lake, as the case might be.

Balnain, from the Gaelic *Baile,* a town or residence. The second part is from the Gaelic word *A in,* a stranger. The old form was *Baile-an-Nain.* The strangers' residence.

Relugas, from the Gaelic *Reidhe,* a smooth hillside, and *Logais,* uneven, rough, full of hindrances and obstructions. The rough hillside.

Pressley, from the Gaelic *Preas,* a furrow or ground cut up by running water, and *Ley,* a meadow. The furrowed meadow land.

Logic is derived from the Gaelic *Lag, Lng,* German *Lucke,* Latin *Laats,* Greek *Lakkos,* a hollow or lake. In topography the word assumes various forms, but the form *Logic* is more common in Aberdeen and Perth than in any of the other counties. In Ireland *Leg* and *Lag* are frequently found. In Ayrshire we have it as Logan, signifying the little hollow.

Brackenhow. – The first part of this word is from the Anglo- Saxon *Braccc,* German *Brake. Braccen* is the plural form, signifying ferns. Icelandic *Bnrkni,* Swedish *Braken,* Danish *Bregne.* Skeat says it was so called because growing on rough or broken ground. The second part is from the Anglo-Saxon *Heah, Heh,* Dutch *Hoog,* Icelandic *Har,* Danish *Hor.* The original sense of these words is bent, hence rounded, knob-like, as a mound or hill. *Hoive* is the English form. The fern hillock.

Glassfield, from the Gaelic *Glas,* grey, blue, or green, and frequently applied as an adjective to local names. Glasgow is said by a Welsh author to be a corruption of *Glas-Coed,* the green wood. We have Glassgreen, near Elgin, which is actually a tautology. The green field.

Chapclhall, from the Latin *Capella,* German *Kapella,* which are derived from the Latin root *Capa,* a hooded cloak; hence a shrine in which was preserved the cape or hood of St. Martin. The word is common in Scotland, and indicates where these shrines were originally erected. Another form of the word is Kirkhill.

Knockiefin, from the Gaelic *Cnoc,* a hill or knock. *Knockie* is the diminutive form. The latter part is from the Gaelic *Fionn,* white. It is also frequently found as *Fin,* Welsh *Guynn.* Perhaps the most extravagant form of this word is found in Phoenix Park, Dublin, and was so called from a beautiful spring well in the grounds. We find it also in Loch Fyne, a clear or beautiful lake. The word signifies the fair or white hill.

Downduff. – The first part of this word is a corruption of the Gaelic *Dun,* a stronghold, a hill fort, the primary meaning of which is strong. By extension it has long been applied to hills and mountains having no fort or stronghold. The latter part of the word is from the Gaelic *Du* or *Dubh,* black. The black hill.

Cooperhill. – The prefix here is from the Gaelic *Cabar,* a height or eminence – as in the phrase *Cabar Beinne,* the mountain top. The word hill appended forms a tautology.

Gervally. – There is an old Gaelic word *Gaertha* (pronounced *Garka)* used to signify a woodland along the banks of a river, literally meaning bushes or underwood. It is found as *Ger, Gear, Gaer,* and *Gair.* The latter part is from *Baile,* a residence. The word signifies the residence in the wood near the river. The local meaning is *Garbh-bhaile,* the rough place of abode or rough farm.

Greens. – The old form of this word was *Grianach,* which was corrupted into its present form about 1724. It is from the Gaelic *Grian,* the sun, and signifies the sunny spot or solarium or *terra Solaris.* The name was usually given to the spots where royal residences were built in Pictish times; hence all palaces built on , sunny hills were *Grcenans.* In course of time the diminutive *an* was dropped, and the form *Greens* was adopted.

Drumine. – The first part of this word is from the Gaelic *Druim* or *Drom,* the back, and cognate with the Latin *Dorsum.* The second part is the Celtic *Min, Men,* or *Maen,* a high rock or the brow of a hill. The hill ridge.

Sluie. – The old form of this word was *Sleagh,* which is the Gaelic for a spear, and in topography is applied to wood, especiallyto tall trees, and is met with in such words as *Cnoc-na-Sleagh, Dail-na-SUagh,* and *Bruaich-na-Sleagh.* The word was first applied from the fact that in olden times warriors used to cut their spears from these woods in a green state, as they were more pliable and less liable to be broken.

Romach, from the Gaelic *Rnmach,* a marsh or quagmire. Another form of the word is *Rumaich,* and the adjective form is *Rumachail,* marshy or boggy.

Tomnamoon. – The old form was *Tom-na-Moine,* from the Gaelic *Tom,* a hill. *Na* is the genitive *of,* and *Maine* is the Gaelic for peat. The hill of the peat moss.

Falkirk is an imported word after the place so called in Stirlingshire. In 1382 it was *Fawkirc,* but the word prior to that date was *Eglaisbhreac.* About the year 1000 it was *Egglesbreth*; in 1160 it was Latinised "*Ecclesia de Egglesbrec" Eaglais* is the Gaelic for church, and *Brcac* signifies speckled or mottled. The Scotch *Faw,* van-coloured, was about the year 1382 substituted for *Breac*; hence Falkirk signifies the church of the mottled stone.

Lynaghonc, from the Gaelic *Linne,* Welsh *Lynn,* a pool, a lake, and sometimes applied to a depression in the ground. *Na* is the genitive *of.* The latter part is from the Gaelic *Gobhainn,* a smith. The smith's hollow or pool.

Aitnoch, from the Gaelic *Aitionn,* broom or gorse. *Noch* or *Och* is the adjectival termination *Nach* or *Ach.* The word signifies abounding in gorse.

Culfairn. – From the Gaelic *Cul* or *Ctiil,* the back or corner. The latter part is from the Gaelic *Fearn,* the alder, and is found as *Fern, Farn, Fairn, Vern, Varn,* and *Varna.* The alderwood corner.

Torchroisk. – The prefix here is from the Gaelic *Torr,* Welsh*Twr,* Latin *Turris,* Greek *Pyrgos,* a mound, heap, or conical hill. We find it on the Contintent reduplicated as in Torres-Torres, the fortification of the mountains, and Turris-Cremata, the burned tower. The latter part, *Chroisk,* is the oblique form of *Crasg,* a cross, which is cognate with the Latin *Crux.* In olden times it was usual among the people of the country to mark the spot where " any Providential visitation took place," or where any great event happened, by the erection of a cross in commemoration of the event. The hill of the cross.

Bowiesford. – The old form of this word was *Bothar,* without the affix *Ford. Bothar* is the Gaelic for a lane, a road, or passage; also stepping stones by which to cross a stream. The English *Ford* being affixed, the word forms a tautology signifying passage.

Tormore. – This is quite a common word, and is frequently met with throughout the country. It is from the Gaelic *Ton;* a mound, a heap, or conical hill, and *Mhor,* big. The big hill.

Stripe, from the Gaelic *Strenp,* strife, contention, a skirmish, or insurrection. The place of the battle or skirmish, or the place of contention. Tradition says that in olden times there was a battle fought in close proximity to this place.

Out/awcll. – This word is composed of three parts, the first, *Out,* being from the Norse *Hant,* a hill or promontory, and is found in Scotland as *Faut, Out,* and *It.* The second is the Anglo-Saxon *Law,* also a hill, and with the former word forms a tautology. The last word, *Well,* is the English for a spring of water. The well of the hill.

Tomcork, from the Gaelic *Tom,* a round hillock or knoll, a rising ground, and the Gaelic *Corca,* oats. The ground suitable for growing oats, which thrives well on rough land, and feeds upon coarse decayed vegetable matter.

Achindar, from the Gaelic *Achadh,* a field or plain, and *Dair, Dar, Dero,* and *Deryn,* cognate with the Latin *Drus* and Sanskrit *Dru,* the oak. The oak wood, field or plain. *Darach* is the adjective form, and glosses *qnercetum,* signifying an oak grove.

Shenval, from the Gaelic *Sean,* old. The application of the word old in topography refers to date of occupation or cultivation, those places first occupied or cultivated being considered as of older date than more recent places, hence the use of the word. The second part, *Val,* is from the Gaelic *Baile,* a town or residence. In this word the initial *b* is eclipsed by its equivalent *v.*

Ardoch, from the Gaelic *Ard,* a height, and *Achadh,* a field or plain. The plain on the height. This word is frequently met with in the topography of Scotland.

Pitnisk, from the Gaelic *Pitt* or *Pitten,* Anglo-Saxon *Pytt,* cognate with the Latin *Putcus,* a well, signifying a hollow. This word occurs frequently as a prefix. *An* is the genitive *of,* and *Uisge,* water. *Uisge* is found in the various forms of *Esk, hk, Usk, Eske,* and *Uisg.* The watery hollow.

Corshelloch, from the Gaelic *Coire,* a hollow or deep gully, and *Seileach,* abounding in willows. It is cognate with the Latin *Salix,* Welsh *Helgy,* Manx *Shell.* The willow hollow.

Achiulochan, from the Gaelic *Achadh,* a field or plain. The second syllable, *l,* is the oblique form of the genitive *an,* signifying *of. Lochan* is a little loch. The plain or field of the little

loch.

Kerrow, from the Gaelic *Ceithreamh* (pronounced *Kerrow),* a quarter. It was a custom in olden times to divide the land in divisions, and the fourth part of that division was called a *Ceithreamh* or quarter. This custom was first instituted during the time of the Columbian monks, and carried on until the beginning; of the eighteenth century, and from it was taken the old Scotch measurement, now superseded by the imperial measurement. We find the word in Kirriemuir in Forfar, the big quarter or the bishop's division of land.

Dorsella. – The old form of this word was *Doireshallach,* from the Gaelic *Doire,* a grove, and *Seileach,* abounding in willow. The willow grove.

Lochallan. – The latter part of this word is from the Gaelic *Ailean,* a green, a plain, or meadow, usually applied to the green plains on the margin of water. The loch of the green plain.

Dava. – Mr. Johnstone, of Falkirk, makes this word to signify an ox field, from *Damh* and *Achadh.* This is not correct, because at the present day, far less in olden times, there is not much agricultural land about the place, the nature of the soil being moorland ? The word is a corruption of the Gaelic word *Dabhach,* a district of country, a lot, or certain portion of land. The oblique *bh* is eclipsed by *v,* as is usual in such words.

Rochouln – The old form of this word was *Rathullon,* and points to a very ancient designation, from the Gaelic *Rath,* a stronghold, and *Ullan,* the old Gaelic for a cairn, but primarily used to signify a tomb protected by a *eromlech.* As is well known, these cromlechs were erected so as to form small enclosures, which were not nnfrequently designated raths.

Loan, from the Gaelic *Lon,* a marsh, meadow, or lawn, and first applied to a wild, untilled, shrubby, or grassy plain. *Lon* also signifies the elk, but it is more probable the former is the correct signification.

Tombain, from the Gaelic *Tom,* a hill, and *Ban,* white. The adjectival suffix here is very common throughout the country. The initial *b* of *Ban* becomes by aspiration *v* and *w,* and is metwith in the forms *Vane* and *Wane, Bane, Bawn,* and its pure form, *Ban.*

Bdvlair, from the Gaelic *Baile,* a residence, and *Blair, Blar,* a plan or field, and by extension a field of battle. The residence on plain.

Renilurig, from the Gaelic *Rcidlie,* a hillside stretch, and *Lurg,* a ridge of hill gradually declining into a plain. Applied in the same sense to the leg of an animal as it tapers downward.

Achnagairn. – The first part of this word is from the Gaelic *Achadh,* a field or plain. *Gairn* is an old Gaelic word for a mountain or a hill, and is cognate with the Slavonic *Gova,* Greek *Oros,* and is found on the Continent as *Hora.* The hill plain or field.

Belnreach. – The prefix here is from the Gaelic *Baile,* a residence. The latter part is from the Gaelic *Riabhach,* grey, brindled, or swarthy. The *bh* is dropped in several districts of the country, and hence the word becomes Reach, as found in this word. When applied to land it indicates dun-coloured appearance or land torn up by running water. The residence on the brindled hillside.

Lougskeach – This is a very old word – one of the few words known to belong to pre-Christian times. The word *Lann* was first applied to a house or dwelling. After the advent of the Christian faith it was applied to a church, and retains that application to the present day, not so much in Scotland as in Wales. It has undergone several changes, so that now we find it as Lann, Lang, and Long. The oblique forms are Leng, Ling, and Lyng. The terminal *g* is a modern addition affixed somewhere about the year 1661. The latter part *Skeach* is also from a very old Gaelic word *Sceach,* signifying the white thorn or haw tree. In the latter word the *c* is eclipsed by *k* in the former. This plant, by its widediffusion all over the country, has given names to a large number of places, and is found in the forms of *Ske, Skea,* as in *Skeabost,* in the island of Skye. The dwelling in the hawthorn wood.

Half Davoch. – For the signification of this word see Dava. The prefix Half signifies a ploughgate of land, or half a measure of land.

Aldrishaig, from the Gaelic *A llt,* a burn or stream, and the Gaelic *Driseag,* the diminutive of *Dris,* the bramble, brier, or thorn. The bramble wood burn.

Sloewhite. – This is a modern word. The first part is from the Anglo-Saxon *Slo, Sla,* plural *Slan,* Dutch *Slee,* Danish *Slaaen,* Swedish *Slan.* The fruit of the blackthorn, resembling in colour the jumper berry, having a purple appearance. The affix here does not mean white, but it is an entirely different word derived from Vitu, wood, and found in the forms of Whit, White, as here, and Wit. The sloewood or the blackthorn wood.

Lochnuan, from the Gaelic *Loch,* a lake, and the Gaelic *Uan,* a lamb, cognate with the Latin Agnus, Welsh *Oen.* As is usually the case, it occurs here in the genitive plural with the preposition of prefixed, forming the word Nanuan, of the lambs. *Uanan* is the diminutive form. The loch of the lambs.

Bantrach is the Gaelic for a widow or widower. The word enters into several place names throughout the country, and indicates pieces of land given to widows free of rent and taxes, a custom which was quite common in bygone times.

Foebuie, from the Gaelic *Feith,* a marsh, a boggy stream, or a stream'flowing through a trench. The latter part *Buie* is yellow, with which is cognate the Latin Eadius, English Bay. The yellow marsh.

Dusach. – This is a corruption of the Gaelic *Ghtthasach,* abounding in firwood trees. It is not often that *g* is eclipsed by *d,* and it can only be accounted for by the eccentricities of different writers before the art of printing, when each scribe adopted his own provincial mode of spelling words. It is found as *Dhus, Dhuis,* and *Dus,* as here. The firwood residence.

Craigroy, from the Gaelic Craig or Carrig, a rock, and *Ruadlt,* red. The red rock.

Burutack. – The prefix here is a corruption of the old Gaelic word *Bryn,* a hill ridge, modern Gaelic Bron, a round hill, and frequently found on the Continent, and in Wales as Bryn, in Scotland as Bron, and the Scotch word Tack, literally a lease of land from the superior, and by extension became to be applied to a farm : hence tacksman, one who holds the lease. The farm on the hill.

Brylack. – The first part of this word is an old word from the Gaelic *Bri,* a hill or rising ground, and is equivalent to the Scotch Brae, to which evidently on the incoming of English-speaking people they added the old word Lagh for the modern Anglo-Saxon Law, a hill, thus forming a tautology. The hill ridge.

Elgin.

14

SECTION 14

XIII.

PARISH OF ELGIN.

THIS Parish is of irregular form, and extends about ten miles in length and six in breadth. Its superftcial area has been estimated at about 18 square miles. The surface of the parish is flat, but the vales of Mosstowie and Pluscarden are separated by a steep hilly ridge, and the district rises generally from the vicinity of the town towards the Blackhills. The only river of any importance is the Lossie, which flows gently through the level lands, but frequently overflows even its artificial banks. In very remote times tillage seems to have been far advanced in this parish, as the scattered facts collected by the writer of the old statistical account from the political and military history cufficiently indicate, and Tacitus writes that the people of Moray do not dwell together in towns but cultivate the land separately, as a fountain, a plain, or grove pleases them. The hilly ridge between Pluscarden and Mosstowie consists of strata of a peculiar hard and pale-coloured sandstone, of which, in 1826, a considerable quantity was exported to London for the building of London Bridge. The chief place of interest in the landward part of the parish is Pluscarden Abbey, situated in the secluded glen of that name. The old names of this parish have been greatly lost, particularly those places near the town, while in the districts of Mosstowie and Pluscarden, a few of the old names still remain, and are mostly of Gaelic origin.

Elgin. – Tradition ascribes two derivations to this word. First from the Dutch *heilig,* Icelandic *heliagr, helgr* – holy, and found as *hely* and *haly,* and *Dun,* a hill or fortress, *i. e.,* Helydun. The second traditional meaning ascribed to is that it comes from *Helgy,* a general of the army of Sigurd, the Norweigian Earl of Orkney, who, in the year 927, conquered Caithness and Sutherland. That the origin of the name is from this source may be dismissed at once as a fable, because Elgin was a town of considerable note before Helgy ever frequented the Scotch coasts, and because Skene in his " Celtic Scotland " tells us that Helgy never came further south than the Orkney Islands. The word Helgyn being in the inscription on the Corporation Seal has had a great deal to do with the fixing or attributing the word to Helgy. Young, in his " Annals of Elgin," although he does not attempt any derivation, says that doubtless it is a Celtic word. Professor Rhys thinks it is pre-Celtic or Ivernian, and others think it is from Elga, a character in the Mythic history of Ireland, and also a poetic name for Ireland. All these sources are purely conjectural, and do not consider the fact that the early inhabitants of the country when the Romans circumnavigated Britain were Celtic. Such being the case, and taking into account the antiquity of the town, we must look to the Celtic source alone for its meaning. Another important fact that must be borne in mind is that the early inhabitants gave names chiefly from the configuration of the place. All primary place names have been given from this source, or from some other natural aspect, and it is not likely that the place would retain the name of a devastator or plunderer, whosesole purpose was to ravage the country, even if the place had not been previously named.

The other forms of the word found are *Ailginn, Aigin, Ailgin, Ailegin, Eilginn, Elginn.* aud finally Elgin. In no case do we find it, excepting on the Corporation Seal, in the form of *Hdgyn,* and how is it that the Celtic terminal *n* has been added to the proper name Helgy ? Does it not look as if the prepositive part of the word had been dropped to make room for Helgy ? The oldest form of the word was *Ailginn.* In Ross-shire there is another place very much resembling the situation of Elgin named Aligan. Both words come from the Celtic Aille, literally signifying beauty, but in topography a beautiful spot, or valley. The termination *gin* or *gan* are Celtic endings, signifying little, or diminutive forms, and is very common in ancient names' Its original form was *can,* where the initial *c* is softened into *g* when affixed to words ending in vowels. The beautiful valley.

Hillhcad. – Middle English *hil, lnil,* Anglo-Saxon *hyll,* Dutch *hil,* Latin *collis,* Lituanian *Kalnas,* a hill, and head from the Middle English *hed,* heed, heued, Anglo-Saxon heafod, Dutch hoofd, Icelandic hofud, Latin caput, Greek kephale, Sanskrit kapala, literally a skull, and by usage a head, or end. The head of the hill.

Rosebrae. – The first part of this word is from Ros, the old Gaelic for wood. The woody brae.

Stripehead. – From the Dutch *stripe,* to plunder, to flay; hence strype, a strip, or stripe, a streak, then greyish or brindled. The head of the brindled land.

Whitehouse. – Middle English -*whit,* Dutch *wit,* Icelandic *hvnte,* cognate with the Sanskrit *fveta,* from *fvit,* to shine. The white house. Latin writers use the word *Candida,* as in candida casa, the white house.

Castlecraig. – From the Anglo-Saxon *Castcl,* Latin Castellum, a fortified place, and the Gaelic *Craig, Carrig* or *Carrick,* a rock- The stronghold in the rock. Evidently an imported name, or if there had been such a place, there are no vestiges left to distinguish it.

Grcenside. – The old form of this word was *Graenside,* which is evidently from the Gaelic *grian,* the sun, and is a feminine noun. The genitive form is greine, and when found appended to another . word it invariably assumes the genitive form. The sunny side.

Clackmarras. – The old form of this word was *Clachmotharach* (pronounced Clachmorrach). The first part is from *Cloch* or *Clach,* a stone, large or small, and is one of the most common topographical root terms in the country. In the English forms we find the terminal *h* almost invariably changed into *k,* and frequently the final guttural is dropped out altogether. The latter part, *Motkar,* is an old Gaelic word signifying a ruined *rath* or *church,* and by extension used to mean the ruins of any building. In modern Gaelic the word is used to signify a high or swelling sea. It will be observed that *ach* is the adjective form. The stones of the ruined building, or the stoney undulating ground.

Coleburn. – *Coll* is the Gaelic for *hazel,* with which is cognate the Latin *Cory In s* and the modern Gaelic *calltuinn,* and when it forms the initial part, as in the word under review, it is usually found as *Coll, Col, Cole,* and *Cull.* The hazelwood burn.

Oldwells. – The old form of this word was *Eldwell,* which was evidently taken from the Anglo-Saxon *Eald,* Middle English old, Dutch *oud,* and allied to the Latin *ad-ultus,* signifying grown-up. The old well.

Stonehouse. – The old form of this word was *Steinhous,* which indicates that the word is Norse, from the German *Stein,* Dutch*Stecn,* Icelandic *Steinn,* Greek *Stia,* a stone, and the Anglo-Saxon *hns,* Dutch *hnis,* Icelandic *hns,* an abode. In the early ages, the primitive occupants of the country built mud and wooden houses, and when stones were used, the houses were given the general name of Stonehouses.

Longmorn. – The old-form of this word was *Lannmaran.* The word *Laun* is from the Gaelic, and signifies an enclosure, a house,, and a church, and, according to Skene, comes from the Latin *Planum,* a plain, as the Gaelic *Ian* comes from the Latin *Plenvs.* The word is more common in Welsh names than in Scotland, and in its signification of a church enters into a large number of names. All the instances known in the north of Scotland apply to church names. The latter part *Maran* is a corruption of *Eran* or *Eman,* a saint who lived in the 7th century. The initial *M,* and *Mo,* and *Ma* are frequently in the Celtic language prefixed to names to signify endearment. These are not found in Kilernan, or in Kiltearn. The church of St. Ernan.

Whitewreath. – The old form of this word was *Whitraith,* from the Middle English *whit,* Dutch *wit,* Icelandic *hwite* – white, to shine. The latter part is from the Gaelic *rath,* primarily a mound or hill, and by extension a round earthen fort or stronghold, a circle, and cognate with the Welsh *rhath.* The white hill, or white hill fortress or stronghold.

Glassgreen. – This is a tautology. The first part is from the Gaelic *Glas,* and commonly translated green. This is its usual interpretation. It is also used to signify grey, or sometimes blue, as in the Gaelic expression *Suil-Ghlas* – a greyish blue eye, but in its topographical application it is exactly as used in the word under review.

Bogicfearn. – The oldest form of this word was *Bogfearna,* then. it was *Boganfeama,* from which latter came the present form. *Bog* is the Gaelic for a *Bog* or marsh. The latter part *fearna* is the Gaelic for alder, and is frequently found in Scotch topography. The alderwood marsh or bog.

Millbowies. – This word has little resemblance to its primary form, which was *Mealbuidhc,* from the Gaelic *Meall,* literally a lump, but by extension applied to a hill, and applied very often in place names. The latter part is from the Gaelic *Buidhe* – yellow. The yellow hill, so given from the appearance presented by decayed moss.

Minbreck. – The first part of this word comes from the Celtic *Min, Men,* or *Maen* – a high rock or the brow of a hill. The latter part is from the Gaelic *Breac* – greyish or brindled. The grey hill.

Cascade is a modern name, and was so called when a sawmill was erected there in order to get the advantage of water power to drive the mill; and as there is a considerable rush of water at certain seasons, the place is well named.

Cowslacks. – The latter part of this word is from the Middle English *Slak,* cognate with the Gaelic *Slochd* – & hollow, and is frequently met with in the form of *Slack, Slag,* and *Slog,* in the north-eastern counties of Scotland. The cow hollow.

Angushome. – The old form of the word was *Angraham,* which is evidently from the Norse *Anger,* a meadow or field. It is not common in this country, but is very often found in Continental topography – and *ham,* a dwelling. The meadow dwelling.

Cockmuir – The first part of this word is from the Danish *Kok,* a heap. Icelandic *Kokkr,* a lump, a ball, Gaelic *Coc,* as *Coc- Shronach* – cocknosed, and the Norse, *Mor, Mocr* – a moor, or hill. The moory hill.

Manbcen. – The old form of this word was *Maenpeen,* which isevidently from the Celtic *Maen* or *Man,* a place or district, and the Celtic *Pen,* a hill – the district surrounded by hills, or the plain surrounded by hills. In the Welsh the initial *m* is frequently substituted by/', and pronounced *v,* and *fan* is shortened into *fa,* and still further into *a.*

Inchallon. – The first part of this word is from the Gaelic *Tunis,* Welsh *Ynys, Enes,* Latin *Insula,* Greek *Nesos.* It frequently takes the form of *Inch* when found inland – pasture land near water. The latter part of the word is from the Gaelic *Ailean,* a green plain or meadow. Both these roots play an important part in the topography of the country, and are found wherever Gaelic has been the original speech of the inhabitants. In Ireland we find the first as *Ennis,* and the second as *Ailian.* The green pasture land.

Thist/eflat. – This is a modern name, and was given on account of the variety of prickly plants which grew in the place. From the Dutch *Distel,* Icelandic *Thistill,* and Danish *Tidsel,* literally a tearer. Because of its abundance in the country, it had, at a very remote period, been assumed as the national emblem of Scotland.

Htnve. – From the Danish *Hoog,* Icelandic *Har,* Swedish *Hog,* a mound or hill – a height.

Whitetree. – The old form of this word was *Coidreih,* which is evidently from the Gaelic *Coidh,* a round small hill, and *Coidhean* is the Gaelic for a barnacle. The second part is from the Gaelic *Reidhe,* a hillside stretch. The two roots form a tautology. The round hillside stretch.

Higlebank. – The old form of the word was *Uchelbank,* from the Celtic *Uchel,* or *Uch,* Gaelic *Uchda,* a height, and we have it in *Ocliiltree,* the high dwelling, and the Ochills, Latin *Ocelli Mantes.* The high bank.

Holl. – From the Scandinavian, *Holl,* an elevation, cognate with the German *Hugel,* and corrupted into wool, as in Woolwich, anciently Hollwich. The high town.

Redaiiie. – The first part is from the Gaelic *Reidh,* smooth, and also used as a noun to signify a level field, and found as *Re, Rea,* and *Rey.* The latter part is from the Gaelic *Davach,* or *Davoch,* and found in topography as *Davat, Davot, Davy, Davie,* and *Di7y,* a measure of land equal to four ploughgates.

Lochiepots. – The old form was *Loguypot,* which is evidently from the Gaelic *Leoig,* cognate with the Latin *I. uluin,* a marsh. The first name of Paris was *Lutetia-Parisiorum,* the marshy land of the Parisii. The suffix *Pots* has been added to indicate hollows or depressions in the marsh.

Croy. – This word is found as *Crote,* which is evidently the French word *Crois,* a cross – Latin *Crucem,* the accusative of *Crux,* a cross. The monks in olden times were in the habit of erecting crosses in places to commemorate some providential events, and iu consequence the word is frequently met with throughout the country.

Sauchenbogie. – The first part of this word is from the Scotch *Sauch,* English *Salig, Salh,* Latin *Salix,* the willow. *Bogie,* the latter part, is from the Gaelic *Bog,* soft or marshy, and has given names to many places. When found as an affix to names it takes the forms of *Boggy, Bogie, Voggy,* and *Vogy,* and by extension sluggish streams are called by the same name. The willow marsh or stream.

Torriston. – The old form of this word was *Torstang,* which is evidently from the Gaelic *Torr,* a mound, heap, or conical hill, and *Stang,* a pool of stagnant water, a ditch. The hill by the pool or ditch.

Callymuck. – The first part is from the Gaelic *Coille,* a wood, and found in various forms as *Coll, Colly, Collie, Call, Cally,* and *Callie.* The latter part *Muck* is from the Gaelic *Muc,* a pig. This is an old word, and the name was given when the animal was running wild in the country. The wood of the wild pig.

Hardichillock. – The old form of this word was *Ardoch,* which comes from the Gaelic *Ard,* a height, and *Achadh,* a field or plain. The hillock was subsequently affixed. The height of the field or plain.

Fosterseat. – The old form of this word was *Fastra,* from the Gaelic *Fas,* growth, hence also *Fasach,* a wilderness. *Tra, Tre,* or *Tref* signifies a dwelling. The recent terminal, seat, is a reduplication of *Tra.* The modern Gaelic is *Treabhair* (pronounced trear).

Overton. – Anciently the word was *Oferton,* from the Anglo- Saxon *Ofer,* Dutch *Over,* Scandinavian *Ore,* a border, boundary, or point. The boundary dwelling.

Torehead. – From the Gaelic *Torr,* a height, with which is cognate Welsh tur, Latin turris, Greek pyrgos. The head or top of the hill.

Mosstowie. – The prefix here is from the Middle English *Mos,* Anglo-Saxon *Meos,* Dutch *Mos,* Icelandic *Most,* Latin *Afuscus,* moss or swamp. The latter part, *toiuie,* has the same signification as *Towie* and *Tough,* parishes in Aberdeenshire, which come from the Gaelic *Tuath,* the north. The north moss.

Stonewells. – The old form of this word was *Steemvell,* from the Dutch *Steen,* German *Stein,* Anglo-Saxon *Stan,* a rock or stone. The spring of water issuing out of the rock.

Hill/iall. – The old form of this word was *Hoill,* which is evidently from the Gaelic *Aill,* a ridge or rock. In some parts of the country it is found as *Faill,* and takes the form of *Foil* and *Foyle,* as in Aberfoyle. The prefix hill was superimposed about the year 1718, and is cognate with the root *Aill,* thus forming a tautology. The hill ridge.

Slackhead. – The prefix here is from the Icelandic *Slagna, Slag, Slagi,* wet or damp, or marshy, and is allied to the Gaelic *Slog.* The head or end of the marsh.

Eldon. – The prefix *El* is the Scandinavian *Hell, Helle, Helge,* and *Heil,* holy, and frequently, as in this case, the aspirate *//* is dropped, and the word is found as *El, Ell, Elg,* and *Eil.* The suffix *Don* is from the Gaelic *Dun,* literally a fortress, but applied to a hill. The holy hill.

Cloddach. – This is a pure Gaelic word from *Cladac/t,* or *Clodach,* a flat stony place, but more particularly applied to the seashore, as distinguished from *Traigh,* a sandy beach. The word is in general use throughout the country, and, when used inland, to the banks of a river or the margin of a lake.

Longhill. – The first part here is from *Lann,* a house or church, also an enclosure. See Longmorn. The church or inclosure on the hill

Redlnll. – The prefix here is the Anglo-Saxon *Read,* Dutch *Rood,* Icelandic *Raudr,* Greek, *Eruthros,* Gaelic, *Ruath,* Welsh *Rhudd,* Latin *Ruler – ied.* The red hill.

Crossley. – The old form of this word was Crosslaw. The first part is from the Latin *Crux,* and plays a prominent part in the topography of the country. They were put up as memorials of great events or monuments. The hill of the cross or memorial.

Tackside. – In the north-east of Scotland the word *Tack* is applied to a farm, particularly a hill farm, and is derived from the verb *Tack,* to take, or to rent.

Blinkbonny. – The old form of the word was *Elankbone,* which is evidently from the French *Blanc,* Anglo-Saxon *Blanc,* German *Blank* – white, and Middle English *Blenken* – to shine, to glisten. The latter part *Bone* is from the Gaelic *Ban,* white, and is found in the various forms of *Bone, Bain, Bane, Bhan, Bhain, Van,* and *Vane.* When the final *e* is sounded, it invariably takes the form of *Bonny, Bonnie.* A tautology.

Auchtertyre. – The first part of this word is from the Gaelic *Auchter, Ochter,* Welsh *Uchdar,* and signifies a summit, but when used as an adjective, it means upper. The Auchtertyre in Perth was anciently Auchterardower, the summit or source of the water, but the Auchtertyre in Ross and Elgin signify the upper part of the land. The latter part *Tyre* being from the Gaelic *Tir,* land. The upper part of, or summit of the land.

Bogentinny. – The old form of this word was *Bacantcine,* from the Gaelic *Bac,* a hollow or bend, and the Gaelic *Teine,* the general word for fire, which in modern names is found as *Tinny.* The kindling of these fires usually indicated some festive assembly, and such places are frequently found in Scotland.

Sourward. – The ancient form of this word was *Scaurwart,* from the Scandinavian *Scaur,* Middle English *Scatre,* Icelandic, *Sker,* an isolated rock or rocky hill, and the Teutonic *Ward, Wart,* and *Warth,* a guarded place, or fortified place. The guarded or fortified hill.

Mayne. – From the Welsh *Maen,* a place or possession, akin to the Latin *Mansio,* a possession or residence. It is found as *Man, Mayn, Mayne, Main,* and *Mains.*

Pluscarden. – In 1461 this word was Pluscarty, and in 1639 it was Pluscardy. These forms point to the word being of Welsh origin, from the Welsh *Plas,* a place, a sheltered place, and alliedto the Latin *Platea,* Greek *Plateia,* and originally signifted a court or square, and *Cairdean,* friends, or tribe, or community. The place or valley of the brotherhood.

Incharnock. – The first part of this is from the Gaelic *Innis,* an island, and pastureland near water. The latter part is from St. Marnoch. or Marnock, which is found in Marnoch in Banffshire, Inch Marnoch on the Clyde, and Kilmarnock. In this word the initial M of the proper name is dropped to make a distinction.

Culbockhillock. – The first part of the word is from the Gaelic *Cul,* the back or other side of anything. The second part was formerly *Buck,* and is from the Gaelic *Boc,* Dutch *Bok,* Icelandic *Bukkr,* Swedish *Bock,* a he-goat, cognate with the Welsh *Bwch,* Irish *Boc.* This word is usually applied to hills, as in the Buck of the Cabrach. Hillock is a superimposed addition. The back of the buck hillock.

Teindland. – The first part of this word comes from the Anglo- Saxon *Teothe,* Frisian *Teinda,* the tenth part. In Scotland certain portions of the landed property in every parish which have been fixed and valued, and from which parish ministers obtain their stipends, are called teinds. Hence Teindlands means church lands.

Mountswift. – The old form of this word was *Maensuith,* which is evidently from the Welsh *Maen,* a rock or stone, and comes through the French *Mont,* which in its turn comes from the Latin *Mons,* a mountain or hill. *Suith* is a Gaelic word for black, and is allied to the English *Soot.* The black hill.

Fywatt. – The old form of this word was *ft- Wid,* and indicates that the word is purely Norse, from the Scandinavian *Vie, Ve, Wy,* when suffixed to words, and *Fy, Fie,* and *Ft,* when prefixed. The second part is from the Scandinavian *Wid, Widr*and *Vitu, Vit, Vat,* and *Watt,* wood. A wood in which there might have been a church or cell.

Stroanhill. – From the Gaelic *Sron,* and frequently *Stron,* a nose, promontory, or headland, Welsh *Trwyn,* as found in such words as Stronachlachar (stony headland), Strontian (the little headland), Sorn in Ayrshire, named from the ancient castle on the rocky promontory, and also Troon and Duntroon. This word is frequently found in Scotch topography. The pointed hill.

Oldshields. – The suffix here is from the Scandinavian *Scale, Skali,* Icelandic *Skjol,* a temporary summer hut, and found as *Sheilds, Sluil, Sheilin,* and *Sheelin.* It is also found as *Scall,* as in Scalloway in Shetland, and as *Gala,* as in Galashiels, as *Scald* as in Scaldwell. The old shealings.

Bogenhernie. – The first part of this word is from the German *Bogett,* a bend or bow, and in topography applied to the bend of a river, or bend in a road, or bend in the configuration of the land, and the German *Horn,* Anglo-Saxon *Hyrne,* Dutch *Hoorn,* a projection or cape, or a valley between hills, or curved like a horn. This is a tautology. The curved valley or land.

Inverlochty. – The prefix here is from the Gaelic *Inver, Inbhir,* or *Inner,* a river confluence, or a creek at the mouth of the river- The Welsh equivalent is *Aber,* and is generally found on the east of Scotland, while *Inver* is chiefly confined to the west. For the signification of *Lochty,* see the parish of Dallas. Ihe confluence of the Lochty and the Lossie.

Lochinver. – For this word see Inverlochty.

Pittendreich. – The first part of this name is from the Pictish *Pitte, Pitt, Pit,* and *Petti.* The letter *p* is not found in modern Gaelic in connection with the names of mountains, but is eclipsed by its equivalent *b,* as in *beinn* and *ben,* consequently all thewords beginning with this letter, such as Pen, Pette, are Welsh. We find the word also as *Pitten,* a hollow, and *Pettyn.* It is allied to the Anglo-Saxon *Pytt,* Latin *Peuteus,* a well, hollow, or cavity. The latter part *Dreich,* is from the Pictish *Druid/ t* Welsh *Denvydd.* The old form was *Drui,* and takes a *d* at the end of its oblique cases, and was borrowed in this form by the English, whence the word *Druid.* In modern Gaelic *Druidh* would be *Druiach,* that is, one who augurs or foretells. The Druid's hollow, or abode.

Dunkinty. – The first part of this word is from the Gaelic *Dun,* a stronghold, a hill fort, and is cognate with the Welsh *Dm.* As an adjective it signifies strong. It also signifies a hill or mound, and under this meaning is found as *Dune* and *Down.* The second part is from the old Gaelic word *Queintibh* (pronounced *Kinty),* a meeting or assembly. The word, therefore, would appear to mean the moot hill, or the meeting hill.

Tyock. – The ancient form of this word was the Gaelic *Dubhag,* from *Dubh,* black, and *Ag,* a diminutive termination, and signifies a stream or pool, or a deep gulf. The small stream.

Batehen. – The first part of this word is another form of the Pictish word *Pette,* which is found in the double forms of *Bat Butt.* The latter part *Chen,* is a corruption of the Welsh word *Cafen,* a ridge, and cognate with the Greek *Kephale,* a head, and by mutation it becomes *Chen* or *Chev,* as in the Cheviot hills, *C/tevin* in York, or *Chen* in Derby. The hollow at the end of the ridge.

Palmereross. – From the Middle English *Palmerc,* one who bore a palm branch in memory of having been in the Holy Land, or a pilgrim. The cross of the pilgrim, or the abode of the pilgrim.

Auchteen. – The traditional signification given of this word is, that it is the Doric of eighteen, but it is difficult to understand how this duodevigintal number has anything to do with it. It is from the Gaelic *Uchd,* a hill or rising ground, and the Gaelic *Teine,* fire. *Uchdteine.* – One of the hills on which the ancient Bealtane fires used to be kindled.

Allarburn. – The first part of this word is from the Anglo- Saxon *Alr, Aller, Allar,* Dutch *Els,* Icelandic *Olr,* Latin *Alnns,* the *Alder,* The alderwood burn.

Chanonry. – The old form was Canonry, from the Anglo-Saxon *Canon,* Latin *Canou, Kanon,* a rod, rule, an ecclesiastical dignitary, and Old English *Rice* or *Ric,* a jurisdiction. The jurisdiction of the Canon.

Gallowcrook. – In many places throughout Scotland where there are, and have been, stone circles, the name Gallow and Oallan are to be found, which names are the Celtic equivalents to the *Hoar-Stones* in England and *Hare-Stanes* in Scotland, and the *Maengwyr* of Wales. These stones were supposed to have been erected as memorial stones or boundaries. For the meaning of Crook see the Parish of Alves.

Hattonhill. – From the Gaelic *Aiteann,* furze, and found in the English forms as *Hattan* and *Hatton.* The furze bill.

Bilbohall. – The first part is from the Teutonic *Bill,* a plain or level spot. The second syllable is the Norse *Bo,* a dwelling. The dwelling on the level spot or platn.

Stenmanhill. – From the Teutonic *Stein,* Dutch *Stecn,* a stone or rock, and sometimes in topography applied to a rock fortress. The second part is the Welsh *Maen,* also a stone – a tautology. The stoney or rocky hill.

Aldroughty. – From the Gaelic *Allt,* a burn, and the Gaelic *Drochaid,* a bridge. The bridged burn.

Fleurs. – From the French *Fleurs* – flowers, and cognate with the Latin *Flos. Floralis,* belonging to Flora, the goddess of flowers.

Haughland. – In Scotland the words *Haugh* and *Heugh, How,* and *Hope,* denote a low-lying meadow between hills, or on the banks of a river or stream; though in some places the word *Haugh* is from the Scandinavian *Haugr,* a mound, somewhat like the cairns so common in Scotland, the former is doubtless the meaning here. The low-lying land.

Bruceland. – From the Teutonic *Brache,* Scandinavian *Brak,* land broken up for tillage, or the ploughed land.

Norriston, both in Elgin and Stirling, is evidently a common Scotch surname, as Horns Law in Ayr.

The Coat of Arms of Forres are not recorded in the Lyon Office.

In a meadow with springing palms the martyr St. Lawrence, vested as a deacon, holding in his dexter hand the Book of the Gospel, and leaning with the sinister upon a bed of iron bars: in the dexter chief the moon increscent, and in the sinister the sun in his splendour.

The motto is – "Jehovah Tu Mihi Quid Deest." St. Lawrence, after being scourged, was grilled alive on a sort of large girdiron over a slow fire during the night between the o, th and toth August, A. D. 258. The Seal and Coat of Arms, which are of great artistic merit, represent the saint standing in a meadow whence are springing what appears to be palms of victory. These and the whole group ought to be tinctured proper. He is fully vested in alb and dalmatic. This dalmatic ought to be red, on account of his being a martyr, and in representation of Lawrence it is very often powdered with flames of gold.

15

SECTION 15

XIV.

FORRES.

THIS Parish is bounded on the north by Findhorn Bay, a large basin of shallow water formed by the meeting of the tide and the Findhorn River; on the east by Kinloss and Rafford; on the south by Rafford; and on the west by the River Findhorn. It is irregular in form, and is 4 miles in length and 2J in breadth. Its area is about 9 square miles. " In point of climate and situation it is inferior to no part of Scotland. The most interesting antiquities are the celebrated " Sweno's Stone " and the " Witches' Stone." The name Sweno would indicate or suggest *Swein,* King of Norway. This stone is a magnificent Runic obelisk of dark grey stone. The stone steps around the base were placed as supports to the pillar by a Countess of Moray, Lady Ann Campbell, about 200 years ago. The stone is 23 feet above the ground, and is said to be 14 feet under the ground. The breadth at the base is 4 feet, and thickness 15 inches. It bears every appearance of having owed its origin to a period of remote antiquity, and is one of the most remarkable in Britain. It is supposed to commemorate a treaty of peace between Malcolm II. of Scotland and Sweno, the Norse king, about the. '

beginning of the llth century, and its traditionary name would eeem to support this theory. Others suppose that it commemorates the murder of King Duffus, in the Castle of Forres, and the execution of the murderers; and the character of the figures seems to favour the latter tradition.

The "Witches' Stane" was that on which the unfortunate beings accused of witchcraft were wont to suffer. When the turnpike road was in process of being made, the workmen broke this mass of stone, but the townspeople discovering this, and wishing to preserve a relic of the bygone times, immediately caused it to be clasped with iron, in which state it still remains. On the south-eastern side of the town is a small glen, known by the sobriquet of Hell's-Hole-Valley. On one of the heights of the Cluny Hills is a lofty Pharos, commemorative of Nelson and the Battle of Trafalgar. The town of Forres must have been a place of some note at a very early period of our history, and is in all probability the *Varris* of Ptolemy. Boethius, so early as the year 535 makes mention of it as a burgh having merchants, who, for some cause, were put to death, and their goods confiscated to the King's use. It was frequently visited by the Scottish kings during the ninth and tenth centuries. Donald, the son of Constantino, was slain at Forres. Malcolm frequently resided in the vicinity, and was killed in 959 at *Ulern,* the old name for Aldeam. King Duffus, as stated above, was murdered at the Castle by Donevald, the governor, about the year 966, and his body, according to Boethius, was buried under the bridge of Kinloss.

Forres. – In 1187, Fores; 1283, Forais. Like all other ancient places, several significations are given to this word. It is supposed

that it is the *Fodresach* mentioned in the Pictish chronicle of 970. By others it is supposed to be from the tribe *Horestii* or *Foresti,* mentioned by Tacitus in his Agricola as occupying this place. By others it is supposed to be from the Gaelic *Far-tns,* signifying near water. And by others that it is from the Scandinavian *Fors,* a waterfall, which is the most probable. The word *Fors,* or the modern *Foss,* was not strictly applied to a waterfall; it also signified a cascade or turbulent water. The combination *Fors* and *ess,* or *ass,* or *es,* forming a tautology, and the old forms of the word, support this signification.

Mundole. – This is a Norse word from *Munde,* or *Mund,* a river mouth, or a valley on the bank of a river. The old form was *Mundal.* The latter part is the Anglo-Saxon *Dale,* a tautology. The hollow land.

Sanquhar. – The old name was *Sancliar,* and is from the Gaelic: *Sean,* old, and *Cathair,* Welsh *Caer,* castle, seat, or fort. The old fort or castle.

Sheriffbrae. – The old form of this word was *Shirabrae,* from the Gaelic *Siar,* west. The west brae.

Chapelton. – From the Latin *Capella,* Gaelic *Capel,* a chapel or church. Church land.

Scourie. – From the Gaelic *Sgor, Sgeir,* Norse *Skaer, Sguir,* or *Sgur,* common names for sharp rocks or mountain or scaur, and allied to the Welsh *Skerid,* and *Ysgariad,* the Scaur.

Bullet/oan. – The old form was *Bullagloan,* which is evidently from the Gaelic *bolg* or *builg* (pronounced *bullig),* and applied to soft places. The latter part *loan* is from the Gaelic *Ion,* a marsh or morass. The word is a tautology.

Mannachy. – The common Gaelic word for a monk or friar is*Manach,* which is the equivalent of the Latin *Monachus.* In Ireland it is *Managh.* The land of the friar or monk.

Greeshop. – From the Icelandic *gn's,* Danish *grus,* Scotch *grise,* a pig. The latter part is from the Teutonic *hof,* Dutch *hoeve,* and frequently found as *hap* and *hop,* an enclosure. The pigs' fold or enclosure.

Blervie. – In 1667 the form of this word was *Blairie,* from the Gaelic *blair* or *blar,* a plain, originally a battlefield. The latter part is the Celtic *ia,* or *ie,* land or country.

Califer. – The old form was *Kaelifart,* evidently from the Dutch *Kael,* German *Kahl,* Anglo-Saxon *Calo,* bald or bare, and the Gaelic *fert orferta,* a trench, and sometimes a grave. The cold bare or wet hollow.

Invererne. – For the first part of this word see the parish of Elgin, and for the latter part *Erne,* see the parish of Alves.

Bucktilly, from the Gaelic *hoc,* a buck, a roebuck, and the Gaelic *tulach,* found as *tullo, tully,* and *titty,* a hill or mound or ridge. The deer hill.

Starlands, from the Scandinavian *Ster,* contracted from *Stadr,* a dwelling place, and is met both in Scotland and Ireland.

Drumduan, from the Gaelic *druim* or *drom,* a ridge, cognate with the Latin *dorsnm.* The latter part *duan* is from the Gaelic *dun,* a stronghold or hill fort. As an adjective *dun* means strong, and as a verb, *dunadh,* it signifies closed, or shut in.

Altyre. In 1450 it was *Altre,* in 1573 *Alter.* Taking the old form as the most approximately correct one, the word is derived from the Gaelic *Ail,* literally a rock or cliff, but more frequently applied to high land. We have allied to it the Gaelic *Alt,* or Welsh *A fit,* a height. The second part is from the Celtic, or

ForreS.

Pictish *trc,* Welsh *tref,* a dwelling, or residence. The modern Gaelic is *trebhair.* The residence sheltered by the high land or rising ground.

Cothall. – The first part of this word is from the Welsh *Coed,* Pictish *Coid,* and variously found as *Coit, Coat, Cuit,* and *Cot,* a wood. The residence in the wood.

Balnafery. – From the Gaelic *Baile,* a town or residence, and the Gaelic *Falre,* watch or guard, and the old form was *Bail-na-fairc.* The place of watch or guard.

Knockomie. – The prefix here is from the Gaelic *Cnoc,* Welsh *Kmvc,* a knoll, hill, or mound. The suffix, *Omie,* is a corruption of the Gaelic *Amaidh* (pronounced Amie), trouble, sorrow, disaster. The hill of sorrow or disaster.

Lingieston. – The prefix here is from the Icelandic and Danish *Lyng,* heather. The latter part is from the Norse *Tun,* Anglo- Saxon *Ton,* an enclosure.

Pilmuir. – The first part of this word is from the Celtic *Pile* or *Peel,* a small fortress, The word is not common in the north of Scotland, but on the border between England and Scotland the word is frequently met with, as also in *Peel* in the Isle of Man. The moor fortress.

Balnageith. – From the Gaelic *Baile,* a residence. *Na* is the genitive, and *Gaoth,* wind. *Gaoith* is the genitive of *Gaoth.*

Clovenside. – From the Dutch *Kloven,* Icelandic *Kljnfa,* Anglo- Saxon *Cleofan,* a hollow or passage between two hills.

Gorskeyneuk. – From the Welsh *Cars,* Gaelic *Car,* Norse, *Ker,* Irish *Corgach,* a marsh, and is frequently found in the counties of Aberdeen, Banff, and Elgin, in the forms of *Corskie* and *Gorskie.* The marshy or wet corner.

Cluny. – From the Gaelic *Cluau* or *Cloon,* a fertile piece of land,. and found as *Clunie, Cluney, Clunes,* and *Clones.* These fertile pastures were the favourite spots selected by the monks in Scot- htnd as places of retirement, and eventually became the sites of monasteries and abbeys, although at first the names of these meadows, in many instances, had no connection with religious institutions. This is, however, more with reference to Ireland than to Scotland.

XV.

KINLOSS.

' I HIS parish is bounded on the north by the Moray Firth, on i the east by Alves, on the south by Forres, and on the west by the bay of Findhorn. It is about 3J miles long, and 3 miles broad, with an area of 10 miles. The ruins of Kinloss Abbey stand near the south-eastern extremity of the bay. The Abbey was founded by David I. in 1150 for monks of the Cistertian Order, and confirmed by a Papal bull in 1174. In 1650 the materials of the Abbey were taken to aid in the construction of Cromwell's Fort at Inverness, and little else than a mere outline of its extent was left. The most distinguished Abbot of Kinloss was Robert Reid in 1530, Bishop of Orkney in 1557, and some time President of the Court of Session, and who had a great deal to do with founding the University of Edinburgh, having begun the fund by which it was built by a legacy of 8000 merks. That he was a high personage in the State is seen from the fact that he assisted at the marriage of Mary Queen of Scots with the Dauphin of France. Shaw, the historian of Moray, tells us that the revenues of Kinloss Abbey at the Reformation, according to the Registrum Moraviense, amounted to $1152, besides numerous payments in kind. The whole of the property belonging to the the Abbey, which included land in the counties of Nairn, Inverness, Banff, Aberdeen, and Berwick, was seized, and one Edward Bruce, a commissary of Edinburgh and lord of Session, was appointed to take charge of the entire establishment, who in 1604 was elevated to the rank and title of Baron Kinloss. In 1633 the ill-fated Charles I. raised his son to the higher dignity of Earl of Elgin, a title still enjoyed by his descendants.

It was at Kinloss Abbey that Edward I. of England, dismayed by the distant mountains of Inverness and Boss, halted in his triumphal march through Scotland, and after staying at the Abbey for three weeks returned southward. It is said that King Duffus, who was murdered in the Castle of Forres in 966, having preserved his life by concealing himself in a covered ditch near the spot, reared a chapel on the site of the Abbey in grateful commemoration of his escape. Boethius relates the matter thus: –

" Killos, in Moravia, nomen habet a fluctibus, qui, praeter omnis naturam, derepente vicino in campo pullularunt, dum Duffi Regis corpus revelaretur. Coenobium, post duo fere secula quam Duffus occubuit, fundatum in memoriam miraculi quod ibidem contigisse memoratur."

Kinloss. – According to Boethius, so far back as the year 966 the original form of this word was Killos, and apparently this form was retained till about 1187, when we find it as Kynloss, and in 1251 another change was made to Kinlos. Dempster, writing of the same event above written by Boethius, gives the word as Kilios. It is evident that the first form of the word was Killos, which plainly indicates that there was a church or *Cell, Cill,* or *Kil* there long before the famous Abbey. This *Kil* was founded by St. Osburn from Dumfries, who, it is said, bequeathed to it the small heritage in Berwickshire, from which at a later date part of the revenues of the Abbey were derived. *Killos* therefore is theChurch of St. Osburn. It is significant that in all the names given after this Saint, if the word Kill *is* written in full, the latter syllable of the patronymic is dropped, and if the patronymic is written in full only the initial letter or a contraction of the word Kill is written, as in Closeburn, or anciently Cella-Osburnie, and Killos, both of which was *Kilosburn* and *Kelosbern.*

Findhorn. – Before the inundation of the sea and river in the year 1701, the old names were *Findhern* and *Findern.* The prefix is apparently from the Gaelic *Fionn,* white, and found as *Fin* and *Fyne* in Scotland, in Wales as *Gwynn,* in England as *Ven,* and in Ireland as *Phoen,* as in *Ventry* and *Phoenix.* For the latter part, *Ern,* see the parish of Alves. The clear or white stream or river.

Damhead. – This is not an old word, and is from the Anglo- Saxon *Damm,* Dutch *Dam,* Icelandic *Dammr,* a mound or bank against water; hence dam, a pool of water, as a milldam.

Struthers, anciently *Strothers,* from the Gaelic *Sruth, Sruthair,* Sanskrit *Sru* and *Srota,* cognate with the Teutonic *Stroum* and *Struya,* a river or flowing water, as in Anstruther in Fife and Westruther in Berwick.

Muttonhole. – In 1617 *Muttole,* evidently from the Anglo-Saxon *Mot* or *Moot,* a place of assembly. The latter part of the word is probably a corruption of hill. The hill or place where foreigners held their courts of justice.

Archies ton. – This is a comparatively recent name, and is a patronymic after a man Archibald.

Scotsburn. – The burn of the Scots or Celts, so called from the fact that a band of Celts retained their position in this place when others were driven inland in the troublous times of the Norse invasions, and is contradistinguished from *Nor-burn* and *No-burn,*

the burn of the Norsemen.

Hatton. – This word is found in the Pictish chronicle of 970, *A than,* signifying the ford of the river, from the two Gaelic words, *Ath, &* ford, and *Abhuinn,* a river. But more probably it is the Gaelic *Aiteann,* the furze, or juniper, and frequently found as *Hattin* and *Hatton.* The juniper field.

Langcote. – The prefix here is from the Gaelic *Lann,* Welsh *Lian,* Teutonic *Land,* an enclosure, a church, or house. Skene says the Welsh *Llan* is from the Latin *Planum,* a plain. The suffix *Cote* is the Welsh *Coed,* or *Coid,* or *Cnit.* The church wood or enclosed wood.

Grange. – From the French *Grange,* a farm or storehouse for grain, which in its turn is taken from the Latin *Granaria,* and with which is cognate the Gaelic *Grainnseach.*

Whiteinch. – The latter part of this word is from the Gaelic *Innish,* literally an island, but applied to low-lying pastureland near a river. The white meadow.

Newton, anciently *Neuton,* signifying the new dwelling. This is a common name in Scotland.

Seapark, anciently *Seaparc,* from the French *Pare,* Gaelic *Pairc,* Anglo-Saxon *Pcarroc,* and German *Pferch,* and signifying an enclosure for cattle or deer, and also an enclosure for the protection of game or for pleasure.

Muirton. – From the Scandinavian *Moer* or *Mor,* Scotch *Muir.* Waste land or heath.

Middleton. – From the Icelandic *Midr,* Dutch *Mid,* Anglo- Saxon *Midd,* the Middle, cognate with the Latin *Medius,* Greek *Mesos,* and Sanskrit *Madhya,* and the Scandinavian *Tun,* Anglo- Saxon *Ton.* An enclosure or town.

16

SECTION 16

XVI.

KNOCKANDO.

THIS parish is bounded on the north by Dallas, on the east by Rothes, on the south and south-west by Inveraven, from which it is separated by the river Spey, and on the west by Cromdale and Edinkellie. It is 10 miles in length and 2 in breadth. The surface is hilly, and the rocks primitive. Near Easter Elchies, at the eastern extremity of the parish, is one of the two celebrated rocks called Craigellachie. The other is in Rothiemurchus. Signals by fire to convene the inhabitants on the approach of an enemy were wont to be made in former times on these rocks, hence the motto of the Grants, " Stand fast, Craigellachie." Near the mansion house of Easter Elchies in a wood is the rural and sequestered Churchyard of Macallan, where a fragment of the church wall is still traceable. Several other ancient chapels or religious houses are said to have formerly existed in this parish, and there are still remains of a Druidical temple. The parish includes the whole of the old parish of Macallan, which was evidently merged into Knockando somewhere between the years 1683 and 1712. No legal record of annexation can be found, but in 1688 they were under separate pastors, while in 1712 we find them under one only. This parish suffered severely from the floods of 1829, an account of which is fully and graphically given by Sir T. Dick Lauder.

Knockando. – From the Gaelic *Cnoc,* Welsh *Knwc,* a hill or mound. The latter part is from the Gaelic *Dhu,* black, and is found as *Du* and *Do,* or *Dow.*

Tomdow. – From the Gaelic *Tom,* a knoll or hill, and the Gaelic *Dhu,* black.

Macallan, anciently *Magh-Ellan,* and St. Colins, a corruption of the former. This is a very old name, found as far back as the time of the introduction of the Christian faith into Scotland. The first part *Magh* is from the old Gaelic, and signifies a plain or level tract of land. It is termed Campus or planities by Latin writers, and found as *Magh, May, Ma,* and *Mo,* also as *Mah* and *Mac,* and in modern Gaelic it is *Mac-hir,* from *Magh* and *tir,* the level land. Then by extension it has come to signify a fertile spot, and in primitive ages churches were built in these fertile spots; so in many places it has also come to signify a church. The latter part *Ellan* is the genitive or oblique form of *St. Fillan.* The name is found in several other places invariably as *Ellan,* as in Killellan in Ross. It is thought the saint was led hither by the fact that prior to his time there was a Druidical temple in the place, being thus a fit place to establish a church for his missionary work.

Dellhallie. – The old form of this word was *Dail-a-bhaile,* from the Gaelic *dail,* Anglo-Saxon *dal,* Dutch *deel,* and Irish *dal,* a district, part, or hollow, and *baile,* a residence or farm.

Borlum. – This is a pure Gaelic word, signifying a ridge or declivity, and also a patch of arable land. It is frequently met with throughout the country.

Overtown. – The first part of this word is from the Dutch *Over, Upper,* and found in the German form as *Ob* and *Ober.*

Dalmoonack. – The first part of this word is from the Gaelic *dail,* a part or district, or a level tract of land, and the Gaelic*Monadh* (pronounced *Monagh),* a heath, or heathy expanse, or mountain.

Bogroy. – From the Gaelic *bog-ruadh,* red bog, so called from the fact that the alluvial deposits consist of clay, iron ore, fuller's earth, and marl.

Kirdals and *Kirdalbeg.* – The first part of this word is from the Gaelic *Car,* Welsh *Cors,* Scandinavian *Ker,* a marsh, and is found in the various forms of *Corse, Cors, Car, Ker, Kir,* and *Keer,* and *dal,* a hollow. The marshy hollow. *Beg* at the end of the latter word signifies small or little. The little marshy hollow.

Tomlea. – From the Gaelic *Tom,* a hill, and *Hath,* grey. The local pronunciation is *Tomliath,* the grey hill or knoll. A very applicable name.

Tomnahera. – From the Gaelic *Tom,* a hill. *Na* is the genitive *of.* The latter part, *hera,* assumes the oblique form *offaire,* to watch or guard, where the aspirate *h* eclipses the initial *f.* The signal or watch hill.

Lynechurn. – From the Gaelic *Linne,* Welsh *Llynn,* Anglo-Saxon *Hlynna,* a pool, lake, and sometimes applied to a waterfall. *Chum* is the oblique form of *earn,* a heap of stones such as was thrown up by the ancient Britons over the graves of their heroes; also a conical rock or mount.

Tulisk. – From the provincial Gaelic *Tuilaisg,* a disaster or a mournful event, or a place of accident.

Cathrinbrae. – The old form of this word was *Cathair-Braidhe,* from the Gaelic *Cathair,* a seat, or house, and *Braidhe,* the face or top of a hill. The house on the top of a hill.

Chtne. – From the Gaelic *Cluan,* or *Cloon,* a fertile piece of land surrounded by a bog. The word is found in the various forms of *Chtne, Clunie, Cluny, Clunes,* and *Clones.*

Cardookhead. – For this word see Cardow. The head of the black rock.

Ddnapot. – From the Gaelic *dal,* a district or hollow, and the Gaelic *poit,* a caldron The hollow or dell of the caldron.

Ladycroft. – This is an old word. " Our Lady " of the Catholic ritual signifies the Virgin Mary, and was so called because this piece of land originally belonged to the Church of St. Fillan. i *Buoldow.* – The first part of this word is from the German *Buhil,*

' j a hill, and found as *bul, bhul, buol,* and *bhoul.* The latter part is *du* or *dliu,* black.

Bishoperoft. – The croft of the Bishop, and indicates, like Lady Croft, land set apart for church or ecclesiastical purposes.

Heathfield – The initial part of this word is from the Middle English *Heth,* Dutch *Heide,* Icelandic *Heidr,* Gothic *Haithi.* Waste land or pasture.

Elehies. – This word is not the same as found in Craigellachie. The old form was *Elche.* It is one of the few words of Basque origin, like *//* and *Ura,* both signifying water, that we have left in the country. The first part is *El,* a town or residence. The second part, *Che,* is a hill. The residence on the hill. The prefix is met with as *Ely, Eli, Ell, Ello,* and *Ole.*

Waulkmill. – The prefix here is from the Dutch *Waleken,* Swedish *Valka,* Danish *Valke,* to press, to full cloth, and allied to the Latin *Uergere,* to bend, turn, incline. The mill for waulking or pressing cloth.

Rhinover. – The first part *Rhin* is from the Celtic *Rhynn,* Irish *Rinn,* Scandinavian *Rain,* a promontory or peninsula, and is found both in Scotland and Ireland in the various forms of *Rin, Rhin, Recn, Rine,* and *Ring.* The second part is from the Dutch *Over,* a boundary, Scandinavian *Eyre* or *Ore,* a boundary or point.

Ballintomb. – From the Gaelic *Baile,* in Ireland *Bally,* originally merely a place, a home, then a fort, a town, and allied to the Greek *Polis.* The latter part is the Gaelic *Tom,* a hill or knoll.

Strondow. – The first part is from the Gaelic *Sron,* Welsh *Trwyn,* a nose, or promontory, and frequently found as *Stron,* as in *Stronfearn, Strontian,* and *Strondeas. Dow* is from the Gaelic *du* or *d/iu,* black.

Bal-na Sco. – From the Gaelic *Baile,* a home, or residence. The latter part is from the Gaelic *Sgoth* (pronounced *Sgo),* literally a gash or cut. In topography it signifies a gully. *Sgoth* is also the Gaelic for a boat; so that the word may either signify the residence in the hollow or boat house.

Ringorm. – For the first part of this word see Rhinover. The latter part is from the Gaelic *Gorm,* literally blue, but applied in topography it signifies green. Green grass is translated " *Feur gorni"*

Brackenhowes. – The first part is from the Anglo-Saxon *Braccan,* Icelandic *Burkni,* Swedish *Braken,* Danish *Bregne,* fern, and allied to *Brok,* sedge or rough grass. *Hnves,* the second part, is from Scandinavian *How,* a hill, Icelandic *Haugr,* Swedish *Hog,* and Danish *Hoi.* The fern hills.

CardoiV. – The prefix here is evidently from the old Pictish word *Carr,* a rock, or rocky land, and it is probable that *Carrig,* a rock, *Cam,* a monumental heap of stones, and the Welsh *Caer,* a hill fortress, are etymologically allied to this word. The latter part is from the Gaelic *du* or *dhu,* black. The name is a very old one, being known as Carrdubh about the time the parish of Macallan was merged into Knockando. It is also, so far as the writer knows, unique in the topography of Scotland. Both the prefix and affix are common, but as a combination no other can be found.

Darglans. – The prefix here is from the Gaelic *dobhar,* water, and is found in the various forms of *dower, dover, dur, dar,* and Welsh *dwr.* The latter part is from the Pictish *Glan,* a shore, a brink, a river side. The water side.

Prescalton. – The prefix here is from the old Gaelic word *Prais,* strong, and by extension a stronghold or fortification. The second part, *Calton,* is *Cailtane,* son of Girim, King of the Picts, whose stronghold was in this parish. The old form of the word was *Pras-chaltane.* The fort or temple of Cailtane.

Gortons. – This is a pure Gaelic word, *Gort* signifying standing corn, and fields suitable for growing corn are usually called *Goir- tanan* in the plural. The singular is *Gortan.*

Corgyle. – The prefix here is from the Gaelic *Coire,* a ravine or a hollow. The latter part is from the Gaelic *Gall,* a stranger. *Goil* or *Gyle* is the oblique form of *Gall,* and the old form of the word was *Coireghoil.* The stranger or lowlanders' hollow.

Caley, Bridge of. – The latter part of this word is from the Gaelic *Coille,* a wood, and the name was borrowed from the Bridge of Cally in Perth.

Rinnifiach. – The first part of this word is from the Gaelic *Rinn,* literally the point of anything, and in topography is applied to a promontory or isolated mountain peak. The second part *Fiach* is the Gaelic for raven. The hill of the ravens.

Tombreck. – From the Gaelic *Tom,*a hill; quite common throughout the country. The second part *Brcac* signifies speckled or particoloured. Hillsides or dry uplands frequently present speckled or spotted appearance. This word is also found as *Brack,* as in Bracklaw in Nairn. The speckled hill.

Gracemount. – This is a modern name, taken from the French *Grace,* pleasing or beautiful, and allied to the Latin *Gratus,* and*Mount,* a hill, Anglo-Saxon, *Munt,* and Latin *Mons.* The beautiful hill.

Garlinebeg. – This word is composed of three roots, (1) *Garbh,* the Gaelic for rough, (2) *Linn,* the Gaelic for pool, and (3) *Beag,* the Gaelic for little. The little rough linn.

Tomore. – From the Gaelic *Tom,* a hill, and *Mhor,* large. The large hill.

Knockandreich. – From the Gaelic *Cnoc,* a hill, mound, or knoll. *An* here is a diminutive. *Dreich* is a corruption of the Gaelic *Draoidh,* a Druid. The Druid's hill.

Garlinemore. – See Garlinebeg. The big rough linn.

Lynes. – From the Gaelic *Linne,* a pool, or lake, and sometimes a waterfall. With which is cognate the Welsh *Llynn,* and Anglo- Saxon *Hlynna.*

Hauglts, found in Scotland as *Hangh* or *Heugh,* and generally denoting a low-lying meadow between hills or on the banks of a stream.

Pitchroy. – The initial *Pit,* found in the " Book of Deer " as *Pette,* signifies a portion of land. It is also applied to a dwelling, and has an equivalent in *Both,* a booth, and so also in the Scandinavian *Bo* and *By.* It is also found in the form of *Pitt,* signifying a hollow, and allied to the Latin *Puteus,* a well. The latter part *Chroy* is a corruption of the Gaelic *Graoibh,* trees or wood.

Strathgean. – The first part comes from the Gaelic *Srath,* a valley. The latter part *Gcan* is another form of *Gen,* an abbreviation of the Teutonic *Magen* or *Megen,* a field or plain. Is a tautology.

Gall. – This word has been used by the Gaels to denote a stranger, usually the Danes, and since then it has been applied tothe English. It is more commonly found with a prefix, but without one it signifies " the strangers' land."

Brunt/ands. – Land reclaimed by burning. In olden times mossy or peaty land was usually brought under cultivation by burning, and in some parts of the country this mode is adopted in the present time.

Cardatiach, from the Gaelic *Carr,* a rock, or rocky, and the Gaelic *Danach,* abounding in. The rocky land.

Dahneonach. – The old form of this word was *Dalmoinach,* signifying the peaty or mossy dale, from the Gaelic *Maine,* peat.

Clune, from the Gaelic *Clnan,* a fertile piece of land.

Culkeen. – The first part is from the Gaelic *Cutl,* a corner or angle, used frequently in the place names of Scotland. There is another word Cul, a back, and in distinguishing between the two it is necessary to know the configuration of the place. The latter part is from *Gin,* or *Ginealachd,* a race or family. Land occupied

by the race for generations. Also from the Gaelic *Cinneadh,* a surname.

Rinnagarrie. – The first part *Rinn* means the point of anything. In its topographical application it signifies a promontory or point of land, and is frequently met with in the place names of Scotland. The second part *Garrie* is from the Gaelic *Garadh,* a dike. The point or end of the dike or boundary.

Corshelloch. – From the Gaelic *Coire,* a deep hollow, and the Gaelic *Seileach,* abounding in willow. The hollow of the willows.

Balmenach. – From the Gaelic *Baile,* a town or residence, and *Meadhonach,* the middle, Middleton.

Balnaglack. – From *Baile,* a town or residence. *Na* is the genitive of, and *Glac,* a hollow or narrow valley. The residence in the narrow valley.

Clashdvw. – From the Gaelic *Clais,* a ditch, and *dubh,* black. The black ditch or valley.

Clashindarish. – For the first part see Clashdow. The latter part is from the Gaelic *dorrach,* rough, rugged. The rough or rugged hollow.

Ballinteem. – From the Gaelic *Baile,* a residence, and *Tuaim,* a mound of earth or stones raised over a grave or in a churchyard, and cognate with the Latin *Tumulus,* the place of the mounds, or *Tumuli.*

Altcosh. – From the Gaelic *Ault,* a burn or stream, and *Giuthas,* fir. The firwood burn.

Lochanstone. – From the Gaelic *Lochan,* a little loch. The word stone was superimposed.

Allacrough. – The first part *Alla* is from the Gaelic *Aill,* a rock, cliff, or precipice, and *Cruach,* a pile, heap, or stack, and in topography a high hill. The rocky hill.

Tomneen. – From the Gaelic *Tout,* a hill or mound, and *Na,* the genitive *of,* and *Enn,* a bird. The hill on which birds congregate.

Tomindugle. – For *Tom,* see Tomneen. The old form of the word was *Tom-an-tabhal,* from the Gaelic *Sabhal,* a barn. The hill of the barn.

Knocknagore, – From the Gaelic *Cnoc,* a hill. The latter part is from *Gobhair,* goats, cognate with the Latin *Caper.* The goat hill.

Claggan. – From the Gaelic *Claigcann,* uniformly found as *Claggan;* topographically applied to a round, hard, dry rocky hill. The adjective is *Claigneach.*

Sheancanop. – From the Gaelic *Shean,* old; but how the word came to be applied in topography it is difficult to say, as one natural feature cannot be older than another. The second word isfrom the Gaelic *Cnap,* a little hill. The old hill. Perhaps the name vas applied from the fact of early cultivation or residence near it.

Corglass. – From the Gaelic *Coire,* a deep hollow, and *Glass,* grey or speckled, and also used in Gaelic to signify green. The green hollow.

Boghur. – This is rather a curious corruption of the older form, *Bogfuar,* from the Gaelic *Bog,* soft. In its original sense it meant a peat moss, or simply a bog, and is found as *Bhog* and *Vogg,* and is equivalent to the word *Fliuch,* wet. The latter part, *Fnart* signifies cold. The cold bog or marsh.

Lekin. – From the Gaelic *Leacann,* steep, shelving ground or the side of a hill. *Leac,* the root, originally means a large flat stone, and is cognate with the Welsh *Llech,* Latin *Lapis,* and Greek *Lit hos.*

Ringorm. – From the Gaelic *Rinn,* the point of anything, a point or spit of land, and *Gorm,* literally blue, but when used in topography it signifies green.

Phaebuie. – From the Gaelic *Feith,* a marsh, and *Buidhe,* yellow. The yellow marsh.

Croftindakart. – *Sagart,* a priest, is only the Latin *Sacerdos,* and is quite common in place names throughout the north of Scotland. The old form of the word was *Croit-an-tagart,* where the initial *s* was eclipsed by the letter *t.* The priests' croft.

Delvenvan. – This word is made up of three Gaelic roots. The first is *Dail,* a valley, sometimes a field, and is frequently found prefixed to other words as *Del.* The second root is *Min,* smooth, where the initial *m* is eclipsed by its equivalent *v.* The third root is *Bhan,* or *Ban,* white, where the combination *bh* is eclipsed by its equivalent *v.* The smooth white field or valley.

SECTION 17

XVII.

RAFFORD.

THIS parish is in the west of the County. Its length is- upwards of 8 miles, and its breadth varies from 3 to 5 miles. Its surface is partly low, flat, and fertile; partly elevated, moorish, and rocky, and the landscape much diversified. About 1840 sandstone and grey slate were quarried. Altyre, now annexed to Rafford, was formerly a distinct parish belonging to the parsonage of Dallas, until in 1661, by an Act of Parliament, it was joined to Rafford. The walls of the old church remain, and in the burying-ground the remains of the Cummings of Logic are interred. The chief mansions are Blervie, Burgee, and Altyre, of which latter, in the beginning of the century, Miss Sinclair wrote : " Our next step was through a scene of unearthly beauty to Altyre,. the most lovely and loveable place you can conceive, belonging to Sir William Gordon Cumming, chief of the Clan Cumming, and representative of the old lords of Badenoch."

Rafford. – The old form of the word was *Raffart,* from the Gaelic *Rath,* and cognate with the Welsh *Rhath,* an earthen fort or stronghold, also a mound or hill. In modern spellings it takes various forms, such as *Raw, Ray, Rah,* and *Ra.* The second part is from *Ard,* a height. We find the word as *Ard-na-Raith,* the height of the fort, and as *Rath-Arda,* the high fort.

Cothall. – From the Celtic *Coed* or *Coid,* a wood, and variously written *Coit, Coat, Cuit,* and *Cot.* In the south of England it is *Quite,* in Wales it is *Goed,* and in Brittany it is found as *Koat* and *Koad.*

Burgie. – In 1240 *Burgn,* from the Gaelic *Burgaid,* or *Burginn,* a muddy stream, from the root *Burn,* water. We have also the adjective *Burgaidich,* signifying muddy or silted.

Scotsburn. – It is said that this place was debatable ground between the Picts and the Scots – that is to say, was claimed by both races or tribes; that finally it came into the possession of the Scots, hence the name.

Marcassie. – From the Gaelic *Marc,* a horse, and *A is,* a covert, a hill, or stronghold. A tilting field.

Granary. – This is a Scotch word signifying a farm or storehouse for grain, from the Latin *Granaria,* or *Granum,* and cognate with the Gaelic *Granniseach.*

Todlioles. – From the Scandinavian *Tod,* a fox, Icelandic, *Toddi,* . German *Zotte, Zote.* Is so called from his shaggy hair. The lairs or holes of the foxes.

Tore, – From the Gaelic *Torr,* Welsh *Twr,* Latin *Turris,* Greek *Pyrgos,* a conical hill or a tower.

Brockloch. – From the Gaelic *BrocJdach,* a warren or a badger's den.

Firmoss. – This is a modern name, from the modern English *Fir,* Anglo-Saxon *Furh,* Icelandic *Fura,* Danish *Fyr,* Welsh *Pyr.* The moss where fallen fir is found.

Phorp. – From the Anglo-Saxon *Thorpe,* an assembly of people, or a village, Welsh *trof,* Icelandic *forp,* Dutch *dorp.* The form *phorp* is evidently of Norse origin, and was applied to a few houses.

Tarras. – From the old Gaelic *Tara,* a height, as found in *Tar/and* in Aberdeen, *Tarradale,* Ross, *Tarrel,* Ross, and *Tarves,* Aberdeen.

Rewerrand. – From the Gaelic *Ruadhan,* a mineral scurf or sediment that collects on the surface of marshy places. Then by extension the land on which the scurf is formed came to be termed *Ruadhfhearann.* The red land.

Starwells. – From the Scotch *Starr,* Norse *Starr,* sedge or rashes. A marshy place where rashes grow.

Blervie. – The first part is from the Gaelic *Blair* or *Blar,* a plain, originally a battlefield. The second part is from the Gaelic *Beith,* Latin *Betula,* the birch tree. The birchwood plain or field.

Breach, from the Gaelic *Breac,* speckled or parti-coloured, an appearance caused by different kinds of vegetation or by the different colours of the ground. Speckled appearance.

Bahill. – *Ba* is the plural of *Bo,* a cow, and glosses *Bos,* with which it is cognate. The cow hill or pasturage.

Tulloch, from the Gaelic *Tulach,* a little hill, and used to denote fertile land.

Cautsford. – From the Gaelic *Cauta,* a lake, or a puddle, or a sluggish stream; also applied to the quince tree. The ford of the sluggish stream.

Bognie, now *Bogan,* anything soft, a quagmire. The root is *Bog,* It is also found as *Bogach* and *Bognachd,* and enters greatly into the place names of the country.

Shogle. – For this word see the parish of Birnie.

Sourbank. – From the Anglo-Saxon *Sur,* Icelandic *Surr,* Danish *Suur,* Welsh *Sur,* course or rough. The rough bank or hill.

Bothies. – From the Gaelic *Both,* a tent or hut, Welsh *Bod,* Cornish *Bos* or *Bod;* originally applied to the huts built in the hills for the purposes of summer herding. *Bothies* is a plural form.

Cluny. – From the Gaelic *Cluan,* a fertile piece of land. These fertile pieces were favourite spots selected by the monks for building purposes.

Wardend. – From the Teutonic *Ward, Wart,* and *Warth,* a guarded place, a watch-tower.

Cassieford. – From the Gaelic *Cas* or *Cassach,* steep, an ascent; also, a difficulty, an emergency, a trying situation. The steep ford.

Lawrencetown. – This is not a patronymic, as is generally supposed. It is from the Gaelic *Lobhar,* a *Leper,* a place for the seclusion of lepers – the land or farm of the lepers. There are also *Leper* lands in Elgin. *Lobharach* is the adjective, and *Lobharanach* signifies one covered with leprosy.

Kilnflat. – The first part is from the Gaelic *Cill,* a cell or burying-ground, or a church. The old form of the word waa *Kil-na-vlait.* The prefix is more frequently found as *Kil* and *Kel.* The second part is from the Dutch *Vleit,* a stream of water, or an arm of the sea or channel. The church or burying-ground beside the stream, or lake, or marsh.

Lochiehill. – For this word see Lochty in the parishes of Dallas and Elgin.

Clodach. – See the parish of Birnie.

Templestones. – From the Latin *Templum,* Greek *Temcnos,* a temple or sacred enclosure, Gaelic *Teampull.* These temples were built by the ancient Picts, or by their priests, the *Druids;* and those remarkable Druidical remains are termed rocking-stones, or in Gaelic *Clachbhrath,* the stones of knowledge, which had apparently been used for the purposes of divination.

Clashdhu. – From the Gaelic *Clash,* a trench, or ditch, or *Fosse,* and *Dhu,* black. The dark hollow or trench.

Reade. – This is the Welsh word *Rkyd,* a ford, and is cognate with the Gaelic *Rathad,* a road.

Farnaley. – The old form of this word was *Fearnaliath,* from the Gaelic *Fearna,* alderwood, and *Liath,* grey. The grey alderwood.

Dobinsbush. – From the Gaelic *Dabhan,* a hollow, a little lake. The shrubby hollow.

Bogawood. – From the Gaelic *Bogach,* wet or marshy. The wood in the marsh, usually alderwood or willows.

Bodnafiach. – The old form was *Badnafiach,* the hill of the ravens, from *Bad,* a tuft or cluster, or little hill, and *Fiaclt,* a raven.

Craigroy. – From the Gaelic *Carrig,* a rock, and *Ruadh,* red. The red rock.

Newtile. – Formerly *Neuille* and *Neutisle,* from the Gaelic *Nuadh,* German *Nat,* Welsh *Newydd,* new, cognate with the Latin *Novus,* and the Greek *Neos,* and the Scandinavian *Twist/e,* a boundary. The new boundary or march.

18

SECTION 18

XVIII.

ROTHES.

THIS parish is in the Strathspey district of Morayshire. Heath-clad hills surround this parish, and limit its agricultural lands to the narrow valley of the Spey, , vhich bounds it on the east. On the hill to the west of the village of Rothes is a quantity of white and red agate, uniformly smooth and finely shaded in its colours, and capable of high polish. On the summit of a round hill in the vicinity of the village stand the ruins of Rothes Castle, the ancient seat of the noble family of Leslie, Earls of Rothes. The castle is one of the most ancient ruins in the country. In 1238 Eva De Mortach, daughter of Muriel De Police, was Domina De Rothes, and in that capacity, in 1263, she made gift by charter of the lands of Inverlochtie to the Cathedral of Moray. It is said that the Leslies had come from Hungary with Atheling, the wife of Malcolm Canmore. In 1457 they were created Earls of Rothes by James II. They seem to have resided at Rothes till somewhere about the year 1620, when they removed to Fifeshire. In 1700 they sold their possessions in Moray to Grant of Elchies. The late Dr. Wilson of Worcester, a native of the parish, bequeathed to it a sum of $500 for educational purposes, the interest of which ought to be enjoyed by the schoolmaster.

Rothes – Several derivations have been given of this word *Ruadhuis,* red water, is given by Shaw. *Roth-ess,* a bend in the river, is given by another. These, however, do not convey a sufficient signification, either as to configuration or situation. The term *Rath* was in very ancient times applied to fortifications, or strongholds, and it is evident from the antiquity of the Rothes fortalice that after it was built it was called *Rath.* In 1420 we find it written as *Rath-es,* that is, the stronghold by the *Ess* or river, or by the waterfall.

Greens. – This is from the Gaelic *Gtian,* the sun. Its literal meaning is a sunny place when applied to place names, but its meaning has been extended to signify a beautiful sunny spot, a green spot, or bower or summer house.

Garbity. – From the Gaelic *Garbh,* rough, and *Aite,* a place, the rough land or rough place, whose present appearance belies the appellation, but which, before the influence of cultivation had changed the appearance, was very suitable.

Whiteriggs. – Dutch *Wit,* Icelandic *Hvitr,* Danish *Hvid,* and German *Weiss,* allied to the Sanskrit *Gveta,* white, or to shine, and Danish *Ryg,* Swedish *Rygg,* Icelandic *Hryggr,* a ridge, or the back of a man or beast. The white ridge.

Corqwhite. – From the Gaelic *Coire,* a deep, round hollow in a mountain, also a deep pool, and a whirpool in the sea. The latter part *Quhite* is from the old Gaelic word *Ceide,* a hill. This suffix is not in'general use, and in the few instances in which it is met with it is much obscured owing to the ancient phonetic custom of writing. The hollow in the hill.

Inchberry. – The initial part is from the Gaelic *Innis,* often taking the form of *Inch* and *lush,* pasture land near a river, and sometimes applied to a large level piece of land. The second partis from the Gaelic *Bearradh,* the top of a mountain, hill, or table land. This place is a fertile terrace on the left bank of the river Spey.

Aikenway. – From the Icelandic *Aik,* or *Eik,* an oakwood, Danish *Eeg,* Swedish *Ek,* Anglo-Saxon *Ac,* English *Oak.* The suffix *En* is the adjectival form, and the word might be anglicised the Oakenway. The path through the oakwood.

Clachbrack. – The old form of this word was *Clachbhreac,* from *Clach,* a stone, and *Breac,* grey or brindled. The grey ridge.

Dundurcus. – The first part is from the Gaelic *Dun,* a stronghold, a hill fort, and also applied to hills, mountains found in England as in Downs, and in Flanders as in Dunes. The second part is a violent corruption of the Gaelic *Tiorcais,* to save from danger, and an old form of the word was Duntorcas. The stronghold of safety.

Sourdenhcad. – The first part is from the Icelandic *Svordr,* literally the skin, rind, or covering, and applied to the grassy covering of the land. *Den* is a hollow, and the word as a whole signifies the head of the grassy hollow.

Or ton. – From the German *Ort,* Dutch *Oort,* Scandinavian *Ord,* a point, corner, and sometimes a place. The dwelling at the point or corner; here at the end of a hill.

Bogincnr. – The first part *Bog* is the Gaelic for soft, and is frequently met with in the place names of the county. The latter part *Cur* is the oblique form of *Car,* & marsh. The word is a tautology signifying the marshy or soft place, *Car* being the first name, and latterly the prefix *Bog* was imposed, or prefixed thereto.

Dandaleith. – In 1612 the form of this word was *Dun-da-lec.* In 1700 we find it as *Dan-da-leth,* and finally in its present form. From *dun,* a hill or stronghold; *da* is the

Gaelic for two, *Leac* is the Gaelic for a large smooth stone. The hill with two rocky faces or sides.

RotheS.

Conrock. – In 1598 the form of this word was *Cunrag,* which is evidently a corrupted form of the old Gaelic word *Cunradh,* a covenant, or bargain, or agreement. The Federal hill.

Achinroath. – The old form of this word was *Ach-an-rath,* from the Gaelic *Achadh,* a field or plain, and the Gaelic *Rath,* cognate with the Welsh *Rhath,* a round earthen fort or stronghold. The plain or field of the fortress.

Brach-hill. – From the Teutonic *Brache,* French *Braque,* German *Brack,* a place for hunting; literally a dog that hunts by the scent. The hunt hill.

Ardeanny. – From the Gaelic *Ard,* a height, and *Canach,* mountain down. The height of the mountain down.

Barluack. – From the Gaelic *Barr,* Welsh *Bar,* Scandinavian *Bard,* literally a summit, but applied to pasture-land on the banks of a river, as *Barr-Tatha,* the old name of Perth, or on heights. The latter part is from the Gaelic *Lothag,* pronounced *Loag,* a young filly. Horse pasture-land.

Piteragie. – From the Gaelic *Pitt,* a hollow, and *Craig,* a rock. The rocky hollow.

Collie. – From the Gaelic *Coill,* a wood. This word enters largely into the place names of Scotland.

Downieha is a comparatively recent name, from the Icelandic *dunn,* 'Swedish *dun,* Dutch *dons,* literally soft plumage, but here signifying grassy. *Ha.* the latter part, is a contraction of haugh, a low-lying meadow. The grassy meadow.

Loanside. – From the Gaelic *Loan, a.* marsh. The side of the marsh.

Drumbain. – From the Gaelic *druim,* a ridge or hill, and *Ban,* white, the white, here brindled hill or ridge.

Sauchenbush. – From the Anglo-Saxon *Salh, Sael,* Latin *Salix,* Scotch *Sauch,* the willow. The hollow or clump of willows.

19

SECTION 19

XIX.

NEW SPYNffi.

THIS parish is bounded on the north by the parishes of Duffus and Drainie, on the east by St. Andrews-Lhanbryd, on the south by Elgin, and on the west by Alves. Its length is four miles, and its mean breadth 2 miles, and area about 8 square miles. The river Lossie traces almost the whole of the southern boundary. The Loch of Spynie, formerly a beautiful sheet of fresh water, 3 miles long by 1 broad, and originally a marine bay, stretched along the northern boundary, but, at the expense of nearly $11,000, has been converted into an unsightly morass – an impregnation of sulphur and iron ore athwart its bed having ruined the hopes which occasioned it to be drained and converted into fertile land. In its lacustrine state it richly ornamented the landscape, and attracted numerous flocks of wild swans, and drew to the woods on its margin the capercailzie or cock of the wood. Spynie Palace, the ancient residence of the Bishops of Moray, the site of whose cathedral, from 1057 till 1224, was in Spynie, now exists in massive, but irreparable ruin near the east end of the bed of the once beautiful lake. It formed a quadrangle of about 120 feet with strong towers at the corners, thus much resembling Dunstaffnage Castle four miles north of Oban. Spynie formerly gave the title of baron to the noble familyof Lindsay. The peerage was created in 1590, and became dormant on the death of George, the third lord, in 1672.

This parish is locally " Quarrywood," from the fact j)f the church and the manse being in the vicinity of the old castle of Quarrywood.

Early in the present century the Barons of the Exchequer expended $900 in planting and otherwise improving a large extent of bishop's land adjacent to the castle, which is Crown property.

Spynie. – In 1295 the form was *Spyny.* Evidently this word is derived from the old Pictish word *Spine,* a hill, or point, or cliff, or rock, and is allied to the modern Gaelic *Spinnean,* a little hill.

Findrassie. – The first part of this word is from the Gaelic *Fin* or *Fionn,* Welsh *Gwynn,* fair or white. The second part is from the German or Dutch *Drecht* or *Dreisch,* fallow ground or meadow pasture. The white meadow or fallow ground.

Rosehaugh. – The first form of this word was *Roshaugh,* from the Icelandic *Ros,* Gaelic *Ros,* signifying *Red,* like a rose. *Haugk* or *Heugh* is the Scotch for a low-lying meadow. The red meadow.

Knockbrae. – From the Gaelic *Cnoc,* a little hill, and invariably found in the English form as Knock, and the Scotch *Brae,* an incline. The hill incline.

Loanhead. – From the Gaelic *Lon,* a marsh, morass, meadow, or lawn. The head or end of the meadow or marsh.

Kintrae. – From the Gaelic *Ceann,* the head or end of, and *Traigh,* the shore. The head of the shore. The word *Traigh* corresponds with the Welsh *Traeth,* Cornish *Trait,* and Latin *Traetus.*

Quarrywood. – The first part of this word is from the Gaelic *Ceathramh,* a quarter, from *Ceathair,* four. The monks in oldentimes were in the habit of dividing the land into sections, and in consequence the word quarter, or *Ceathramh,* is frequently met with in the place names of Scotland. The quarter wood.

Myreside, from the Gaelic *Maor,* Irish *Maeir,* an officer of justice, a *Bailiff* or messenger, and found as *Mnyr, Moy re,* and *Myre.* In olden times the word was applied to factors and ground officers. The bailiffs land.

Aldroughty. – From the Gaelic *Ault* or *Alt,* a stream, and found as *Ald, Auld, Allt,* and *droichead,* a bridge. The origin of stone bridges may be approximately fixed in the eighth century, as the fourteenth Abbot of lona from the years 726 to 752 was *Cilline,* who was surnamed *Droichteach* – that is, bridge-maker – from his being the first to build bridges in Scotland. Many places throughout the country take their names from this word.

Terchick Burn. – From the Gaelic *Teora,* a boundary. The oblique form is *teorsag,* and the genitive is *teorann.* The terminal *ick* is a corruption of *uisge,* water; the water boundary or the boundary burn. It is found as *torick* and *teorsag,* also as *deor sag.* The root or literal meaning is *deor,* a drop or small quantity of water.

Seroggiemill. – From the Gaelic *Sgrog,* a kilne, or place for shrivelling grain; *Sgrogadh,* the act of shrivelling. The mill for grinding shrivelled or dried grain.

Laverock Loch. – The gurgling noise made by running water was in ancient times termed *Labhairach,* from the root *Labhair,* to speak, and doubtless *Laverock* is a corruption of this old expression, and by extension it was applied to a muddy place as

Labaran and *Labar.* We find it also as *Lowrach* and *LourisA.* On the Continent it is found as *Labarus,*

Surradale. – From the Dutch *Swoord,* Icelandic *Svordr,* German *Schwarte,* a sward, and *dalr,* a dale. The green dale or valley sward.

20

SECTION 20

XX.

ST. ANDREWS-LHANBRYD.

THIS parish now includes what were formerly two independent parishes – that of St. Andrews, which was the southern and western part of the present parish, and Lhanbryd, the eastern portion. The two parishes were united in 1781, and in 1796 a new church was built midway between the old churches, about a mile to the north-west of the village of Lhanbryd. The old name of St. Andrews was *Kil-Ma-Lemnoc,* which is at the present day known as *Kil-Molymock.* Up to the present time these old churches retain the names of their founders, to which are either prefixed or suffixed the words *Kill* and *Teampull,* both signifying church. The latter is often contracted into *Tc* or *Ty.* The latter is not common in Scotland, having given place to *Kil* and *Lihan,* the former frequently found and the latter in few cases. It is evident that the name of the monk or saint after whom the church was called has been greatly obscured. St. Molaga, or as he was sometimes called *Molochein,* was born near Cork in Ireland, and after establishing a monastery at a place called *Tulachmin* near Cork, he came to the north of Scotland, thence to Wales. He then became the patron saint of the north of Scotland and Bishop of Lismore and Argyle. A great many churches throughout Scotland were called after him. He was known in Scotland as *Moluag,* and subsequent writers have written it as *Molowok, Milauk,Moluoc, Malogue, Mullag,* and in Latin *Molingus, Mollumoc,* and *Mokmoc.* He died on 20th January, 664. The original name was *Luag* or *Lochein,* and as we are told in Irish histories of these saints the syllables *mo* (my) and *do* or *da* (thy) were frequently prefixed to the names of saints as terms of endearment or reverence, and are now substituted by the term *Rev.,* while the diminutives *an, in,* and *og* and *oc* were affixed. These additions very often greatly changed the names, and those who are not acquainted with the uses of these superimposed syllables are apt to be misled. The land which belonged to this church included Linkwood and Barmuckity, and extended in direction northwards on both sides of the Lossie to the shores of the Moray Firth below Inchbroom.

Lhanbryd. – The first part of this word is Gaelic *Lann,* Welsh *Llau,* and Teutonic *Land,* originally an enclosure, a church, a house. Its signification in Scotland and Wales is strictly confined to church, but in Ireland it signifies a house as well. About the middle of the fifth century there were fifteen holy women in Ireland, who were distinguished by the name of Brigit. The most eminent of them was Bridget, the daughter of Dubhthaig, who lived in the province of Leinster, and who was thus descended from Fuathnairt, a famous prince, and brother to the renowned Conn, the hero of the hundred battles. The character of this pious woman extended not only throughout the whole of Ireland, but throughout the whole of Europe, and the chronicles of the Irish saints tell us that many churches were founded by her and in honour of her in Scotland. She was also called *St. Ite* or *Ide,* but as patron saint of the northern and western portion of Scotland she is best known as St. Bridget, and was succeeded by St. Moluag.

Tiendland Well. – The first part is the old legal Scotch term for the Biblical term *Tithe,* and is cognate with the Icelandic *Tiund,* Swedish *Tiende,* a tenth part. The part of the land allocated for the upkeep of the clergy, or commonly church land.

Crauloch. – From the Gaelic *Cranulach,* woody, trees, a woody place. The word also signifies a *Teal,* or web-footed waterfowl of the duck family, but the former is the more likely correct meaning.

Waulkmill. – For this word see the parish of Cromdale. The mill for pressing or fulling cloth.

Bannuckity. – The old form of this word was *Barmucdhach,* and signifies the top of the undulating ground; from the Gaelic *Bar,* the top, and *Afucach,* little hills or knolls.

Coxton. – This is a patronymic word, derived in the original from the Italian *Cocca,* the notch of an arrow; whence also *Coccare,* to fit an arrow on the bowstring; whence also the word *Cock,* a gun, by transference of the old archery term, an archer became to be called *Cox,* and a stronghold *Coxton,* and there are the ruins well preserved of such a tower in this place.

Harestanes. – From the Icelandic *Heri,* Swedish *Hare,* the common field animal, so called because it has a divided upper lip. *Harestanes* therefore signifies a boundary wall, with openings between the stones, just as the common Scottish bluebell is called *Harebell,* on account of the notches in the bell lip.

Caleots. – This is a tautology from the Gaelic *Coill,* a wood, and the Welsh *Coed,* also a wood, and variously written *Coit, Coat, Cuit,* and *Cot,* and found on the Continent *Koat, Koad,* and *Goed.*

Darkland. – The old form of this word was Borland, which signifies the watery or marshy land from the Gaelic *Dnr* or *Dobhr,* cognate with the Welsh *Dwfr, Dwr,* and Basque *Dour,* water.

Pitgaveny. – The first part of the word is from the Welsh orBrythonic, and commonly used in olden times by the Picts. The Gaelic equivalent *is Both,* Cornish *Bod,* and the three forms, *Pit, Both,* and *Bod,* signify a tent, booth, or hut. This prefix, *Pit,* is not found in pure Gaelic. The word is found variously written as *Pit, Pitte, Petti, Pete,* and *Petty.* Its original meaning was supposed to be a piece of land, but in the " Book of Deer" its signification distinctly points to a place of residence, and the latter is the signification used in the word Pitgaveny. The affix *Gaveny* is clearly a corrupted form of the original *Guanan,* 1200 *Guane,* 1260 *Guaenan,* and 1421 *Gobhain.* The prefix *Both* was primarily attached, and we find the word as *Bothguanan* in 1175, *Bothguane* in 1190, and *Bothguanan* in 1300. The Smith's residence or abode. It must have been after the time that Shakespeare wrote the tragedy of *Macbeth* that the word was changed to Pitgaveny. Dr. M'Lauchlan (late of the Free Gaelic Church, Edinburgh) thinks that *Boath* in Nairnshire is the *Bothgownan* of the dramatist, but this cannot be, as we now know the heath of Hardmoor, celebrated as the place in which Macbeth was met by the weird sisters while he journeyed from Inverness to meet King Duncan at Forres, to be west of *Bothgownan,* and Skrine tells us that it is three miles east of Elgin, so that there is now little doubt that Pitgaveny is the famous *Bothgownan.*

Bogton. – From the Gaelic *Bog,* soft or marshy. The farm or residence near the marsh or moss.

Cranmoss. – For this word see Cranloch in this parish.

Hatton. – For this word see the parish of Speymouth.

Lesmurdie. – The old form of this word was Losmurdy. The first part is evidently from the old Gaelic *Lios, Lis,* or *Les,* a circular mound or entrenchment or earthen fortification, and *Mordha,*great, eminent. The great stronghold, or the residence of the great man.

Troves. – The old name was *Trover.* It is said that at one time this place was disputed property, and that an action at law was raised to decide the question; hence the name from the French *Trouver,* to find. The finding of property.

Pittenseir. – For the first part of this word see Pitgaveny. The latter part is the Gaelic *Saor,* a carpenter. Some suppose it is from *iar,* west, but the old form was *Pit-an-taor,* where in the modern name the *t* has been properly eclipsed by *s.*

Templand. – From the Gaelic *Tcampull,* a church, cognate with
the Latin *Templum,* and Anglicised *Temple* – Church land.

Cotts. – For the meaning of this word see Galoots. The woody place.

Sheriffston. – The oldest form of the word was *Schereston,* then *Sherraston, Sherrachton.* The general idea is that it simply signifies the sheriff's dwelling, While not disputing this without positive proof to the contrary at hand, we know that the monks in olden times were in the habit of dividing the land into portions, such as *Trichas, Bailebiataighs,* and *Seisreachs,* which latter was an extent of land that could be ploughed by six horses in one year, and throughout the country are many places called *Baile-an- tseisreach,* which might be Anglicised *Sherrachston,* and in the former divisions of this parish the land was similarly divided.

Oldshields. – From the Scandinavian *Sheal, Shiel, Shielin, Sheelin,* Icelandic *Skjol,* Swedish *Skjul,* a shelter, a cover, a shed or hut, usually built for the purposes of summer herding. The old huts.

Inchbroom. – From the Gaelic *Innis,* often taking the form of *Inch* and *Insh,* signifying an island or land near water. The plainof the broom, which abundantly grows along the southern shores of the Moray Firth.

Scarfbanks. – From the Gaelic *Sgarbh,* the cormorant, Scotch *Scarf* and *Scart.* The resort of the cormorant.

Gordonsward. – The latter part is from the Teutonic *Ward, Wart,* or *Warth,* a guarded place or watch-tower. The watch- tower of the Gordons.

Lochnabo. – The latter part of this word is from the Gaelic *Bo,* cognate with the Latin *Bos,* and in a Latin manuscript it is found as *Lacus Bovis.* The loch of the cows.

Erroll. – From the Gaelic *Ar,* land, or, literally, ploughed land, and *Rcile,* pebbles, stones. The pebbly or stony land.

Forsterseat. – The old form of this was Foresterseat, hence the name. The forester's place or farm.

Sauchenburn. – The willow burn.

Clatterinbriggs. – The old form was *Cladernbrigg,* from the Welsh *Cladd,* an embankment, or dyke, or ditch. The bridge over the ditch.

Gillevorside. – From the Gaelic *Geillmhor,* yielding, submission. The act of doing penance, obedience. This hill is sometimes called the confessor's hill.

Leuchars. – This is the Welsh *Llwch,* a lake or marsh, and the Gaelic *Ar,* ploughed land. The soft or wet cultivated land.

Pitairlie. – For the first part see Pitgaveny. The latter part is the English early, so given from the fact that it is one of the first farms in Scotland on which the crops ripen.

21

SECTION 21

XXI.

SPEYMOUTH.

THE parish of Speymouth occupies the north-east corner of Elginshire, and is bounded on the east by the river Spey, from which it gets its name. It is 6$ miles long, and has a mean breadth of 1J miles, and consists of the suppressed parishes of Essil and Dipple, which were united into one in 1743.

Essil was the lower, or nearer the sea, of the two old parishes, and is from the Gaelic *losal,* low or lowlying. It is also found as *Iseal, Eeshal,* and is frequently found in topography, as in Essel- mount, the low mountain, Moysel Magh-iosal, the low plain.

Dipple was an ancient rectory, and comprehended the southern or highland part of the parish. The church of Dipple, now demolished, was dedicated to the Holy Ghost, but the burying- ground is still in use. At the style of the churchyard there formerly stood a small house called the " House of the Holy Ghost," around which the people walked with the corpse at burial, which custom was strictly observed until the house was demolished. The word is evidently from the old Gaelic word Diopal, literally signifying the side of the roof of a house, or the side of a hill. The two were thus called upper and lower, a very appropiate appellation as regards the configuration of both.

Lyne. – From the Gaelic *Linne,* Welsh *Llynn,* a pool, lake, and often a pool of stagnant water, hence a hollow.

Ward, Wart, and *Warth,* Icelandic *Vordr,* a watchtower, beacon, or a guarded place, Anglo-Saxon *Waerdian,* German *Warten,* thence *Waering,* a fortification.

Orbliston. – The first part of this word is the Scandinavian *Ord,* a point or corner, and on account of the initial letter of the affix the *d* has been supplanted or eclipsed by *b.* The second part is from the Teutonic *Lyst,* applied in topography to a large house or mansion. The house or dwelling at the point or corner of the rising ground.

Mosstodlach, – From the Icelandic *Mosi,* Swedish *Alossa,* Danish *Mos,* moorland, and the Gaelic *Tudlach,* a heap, and applied to places having irregularities on the surface. The irregular moorland.

Dellachapple. – For this word see the parish of Cromdale.

Trochelhill. – For this word see Trochail, in the parish of Birnie.

Whinnyhaugh. – Middle English *Whynnc* or *Quyn,* Welsh *Chwyn,* gorse, and haugh, a low-lying meadow.

Birniestripe. – The first part of the word is from the Welsh *Bron,* Gaelic *Broinn,* the side of a hill. The second part is from the Dutch *Strijpe,* modern English *Strijpe,* a streak. The striped or streaked hillside.

Garmouth. – The old form of this word was Garmach, from the Gaelic *Garbh,* Welsh *Garw,* rough, and *Mach,* outlet or mouth. The rough outlet or mouth of the river Spey. Very descriptive of the place.

Blinkbonny. – The first part of this word is from the Dutch *Blinken,* Danish *Blinke,* Swedish *Blinka,* and cognate with the Greek *Phlegein,* to burn, to shine, with which also is allied the French *Blanc,* Italian *Blanco,* white, and bonny, fair, or beautiful. The beautiful spot. See parish of Dyke and Moy.

Stynie. – From the Dutch *Steen,* German *Stein,* rocky or stony ground.

Bawds. – For this word see the parish of Boharm.

Corskie. – The old form of the word was *Coruisk,* which is a contraction of *Coire-Uisge.* The watery hollow or *Corrie.* This word is frequently met with in topography.

Corsehill. – This is a corruption of Crossbill, upon which, at the time of the Norse invasion, in the Moray Firth, was erected a cross to commemorate some noticeable event.

Deanshillock. – The old form here was Daneshillock, another of the hills on which some memorial of a conflict with the Norsemen was erected.

Balnacoul. – From the Gaelic *Baile,* a town, village, or residence, and *Coille,* wood. The village in the wood.

Hatton. – For this word see the parish of Kinloss. From the Gaelic *Aiteann,* furze or juniper.

Mannochburn. – The word *Mannoch* is the Gaelic for *Monk* or friar, and is perhaps an adaptation of the Latin *Monachus,* whence the English Monk. It plays an important part in the topography of the country, and is also frequently met with in Wales. The word for a nun is *Cailleach,* from the Gaelic *Caille,* a veil. The veiled woman.

Redburn, – Dutch *Rood,* Middle English *Reed,* Icelandic *Randr,* Swedish *Rod,* Goth *Rands,* Greek, *Eruthros,* Welsh *Rhudd,* Latin *Ruber,* Gaelic *Rnadh,* English Red.

Reddish or fox-coloured, and found Anglicised as *Roy, Roe.* In is extensively met in the formation of place names.

22

SECTION 22

XXII.

URQUHART.

THIS parish stretches along the Moray Firth from the Spey to the Lossie, without any creek or landing place, and in olden times, as now, water was scarce. The Loch of Cots, formerly a conspicuous feature, has been completely drained. The mineral well of Fintan has had about the beginning of the century some provincial fame as a medicinal spa, but its waters, having been analysed, were found not to possess any of the qualities attributed to them. The Abbey Well, the fountain which supplied the monks with water, marks the site of a demolished ancient priory built in 1125 by David I., and made a cell of the Abbey of Dunfermline. Its endowments, the lordship of Urquhart, the lands of Fochabers, other lands in Moray, and part of the fishings on the Spey, were distributed among patriots and Court favourites at the Reformation. Previously, however, the priory had decayed when disunited from Dunfermline in the fourteenth century, and almost suppressed by its union to Pluscardine, The insurgents of Moray in 1160 were met in the moors of Urquhart by the King's army, and were defeated with great slaughter.

Urquhart. – The local meaning given to this word is that it is the Gaelic words *Oire,* a coast or border, *Fad,* long, and *Amhuinn,* a river. This is not so. In the writings of Adamnan it is*Airchartan,* in 1100 Urchard, in 1287 Urquhart, and Owrchard. It will be observed that in subsequent forms to that of Adamnan's the terminal *an* is dropped. In Pictish times *ar* or *air* was land, and *Ceartan* or *Ceartain* was friends, or tribes; then *Airceartan* would mean the tribal lands. The modern Gaelic for *Ceartain* is *Cairdean,* which is strictly confined to signify friends or relations, and we find the same word doing duty in Pluscardine, where the *t* has been eclipsed by *d,* as also in the Kincardines throughout Scotland. It was an ancient custom to divide the land among tribes in this manner.

Muir. – From the Scandinavian *Mor* and *Moer,* Scotch *Muir.* Waste land or heath.

Clockeasie. – The first part of the word is from the Gaelic *Clach, Cloch,* a stone, and *losa,* the Saviour. The old form of the word was *Clach-Isa,* and signifies the same as *Clach N'iobairt* in Perthshire. The stone for offering a sacrifice to the Saviour.

Binns. – The old form of the word was *Druimbinns.* The prefix was omitted about 1700, and the local signification is little hills or knolls, but it is known that the ridge is one of the places selected by the Missionaries of lona for worship, and particularly for the singing of their hymns; hence *Druimbinneas,* the hill ridge of melody, from the Gaelic *Binneas,* melody.

Cranloch. – For this word see the parish of St. Andrews Lhan- bryd. The woody place.

Triepland. The old form of the word was *Thriat/and,* which is evidently the Gaelic *Triath,* a lord, noble, or chief. The land of the noble or chief.

Folds. – Anglo-Saxon *Fald,* also *Falod* and *Falud,* and allied to the Icelandic *Fjol* and *Fjalor,* an enclosure or a pen for sheep or cattle.

Lochs. – Where there was once a loch which *is* now completely drained, and the site agricultural land.

Waterscot. – Middle English, *Cote,* Dutch *Kot,* Icelandic *Kut,* a small dwelling; hence *Cottar,* or *Cott-er,* and *Cott-age.* The small dwelling by the water.

Fernyfield. – Anglo-Saxon *Fearn,* Dutch *Varen,* Sanskrit *Parna,* a family of cryptogamic plants. The field abounding in ferns.

Finfan. – The prefix here is from the Gaelic *Fin* or *Fionn,* Welsh *Gwynn,* fair or white, and the Latin *Fanum,* a temple or church, having the ultimate syllable dropped. The white church or place of worship.

Innes. – This is a patronymic name.

Leuchars. – From the Gaelic *Fleuch,* wet or marshy, and *Ar* or *Air,* land. The wet or marshy land. The initial/is omitted in the adjectival form.

Meft, from the Gaelic *Maithe,* a chieftain, a noble, ruler, or hero. This is elevated ground on which was once a house belonging to some personage of importance.

Elginshill. – For this word see Elgin.

Speylaw. – For the first part of this word see Spey. The latter part is from the Anglo-Saxon *Hleaw,* a hill, and cognate with the Irish *Lagh.* The hill overlooking the Spey.

Unthank. – For this word see the parish of Duffus.

Burnie Stripe. – A strip of land along the course of a small stream.

Jointure. – This is a modern name, and signifies a community or land held conjointly.

Brandston. – From the Icelandic *Brandi;* Dutch *Brand,* a burning of wood. The beacon place or hill.

Broomhill. – See the parish of Cromdale.

. – *The* old form was Wellfield. The field of the well or sprng.

Kenneth's Mount. – The old form of this word was *Cnoc-coinneach,* the meeting hill, and was once called the Moothill, as *Maud* in Aberdeen. Meeting.

Malverston (pronounced Maverston). – From the Welsh *Mawr,* Gaelic *Mor,* great. The chief's town, or residence of the great man.

Cappieshill – From the Gaelic *Capa,* a hill top, the old form being *Capa Hill,* the hill top.

Corbiewell. – Scotch for raven or crow, Danish *Korp,* Latin *Corvus,* French *Corbel.* The well of the raven. Locally called the freebooter's well.

Glad Hill. – From the Anglo-Saxon *Gled,* a kite, or a rapacious bird, so called from its gliding or hovering motion in the air. Dutch *Glijden,* Swedish *Glida,* German *Gleiten.* The kite hill.

Lochnabo. – See the parish of St. Andrews Lhanbryd.

Crarimoss. – From the Gaelic *Cran,* a lot. The lotted moss land. - *Slintack.* – From the Gaelic *Slinn,* stones or slate.

Slinntag. – The stony or slate hill.

Bauds. – From the Gaelic *Bad,* a little knoll, or tuft, or wood.

Ballisland. – The old form was *Bailies'* Land. Bailie is a Scotch word signifying a factor or ground officer.

Tippertait. – From the Gaelic *Tobair,* a well, also, a hollow, and the Scandinavian *Thveit, Thwaite,* a cleared piece of land, and allied to the Danish *Tvede,* a bare piece of land. The cleared hollow land.

Kempson. – The old form of the word was *Knapan,* a little hillock, allied to the Scandinavian *Knap, Knof,* and Gaelic *Cnap.*It is difficult to make out how the word was changed to its present form.

Doulsbnrn. – From *Duil* or *Tuil* Water. The streamlet.

Corskie. – For this word see the parish of Speymouth.

Counagedale. – For this word see the parish of Abemethy.